中国科学院大学
研究生教材系列

学科英语写作教程

化学

Writing a
Research Paper in
Chemistry

总主编 ◎ 高　原　张红晖
主　编 ◎ 杜　朋

清華大学出版社
北京

内 容 简 介

本教程旨在帮助化学专业的同仁有效提高英文论文写作水平，介绍了学术论文写作的特点、要点，以及自建语料库的方法及其基本应用，通过课前引入、教学活动、常用表达积累等环节，循序渐进引导学生发现、学习并掌握各章节的重难点。附录部分还提供了常用化学词缀表、示例论文等拓展学习资源。本教材教学目标明确，学科特色鲜明，既可作为化学相关专业硕博研究生学术英语写作教材，也可作为学术论文写作的参考工具书。

版权所有，侵权必究。举报：010-62782989，beiqinquan@tup.tsinghua.edu.cn。

图书在版编目（CIP）数据

学科英语写作教程. 化学／高原，张红晖总主编；杜朋主编. — 北京：清华大学出版社，2022.11

中国科学院大学研究生教材系列

ISBN 978-7-302-62092-1

Ⅰ. ①学… Ⅱ. ①高… ②张… ③杜… Ⅲ. ①化学—英语—写作—研究生—教材 Ⅳ. ①H319.36

中国版本图书馆 CIP 数据核字（2022）第 198307 号

责任编辑：刘细珍
封面设计：李尘工作室
责任校对：王凤芝
责任印制：曹婉颖

出版发行：清华大学出版社
　　　　网　　址：http://www.tup.com.cn, http://www.wqbook.com
　　　　地　　址：北京清华大学学研大厦A座　　邮　　编：100084
　　　　社 总 机：010-83470000　　邮　　购：010-62786544
　　　　投稿与读者服务：010-62776969, c-service@tup.tsinghua.edu.cn
　　　　质量反馈：010-62772015, zhiliang@tup.tsinghua.edu.cn

印 装 者：三河市君旺印务有限公司
经　　销：全国新华书店
开　　本：185mm×260mm　　印　张：8.75　　字　数：196千字
版　　次：2022年11月第1版　　印　次：2022年11月第1次印刷
定　　价：55.00 元

产品编号：091877-01

总　　序

2020年11月，教育部新文科建设工作组发布的《新文科建设宣言》指出："文科教育融合发展需要新文科。新科技和产业革命浪潮奔腾而至，社会问题日益综合化复杂化，应对新变化、解决复杂问题亟需跨学科专业的知识整合，推动融合发展是新文科建设的必然选择。进一步打破学科专业壁垒，推动文科专业之间深度融通、文科与理工农医交叉融合，融入现代信息技术赋能文科教育，实现自我的革故鼎新，新文科建设势在必行。"学科英语是外语学科和专业学科相互交叉、彼此融合的产物，符合国家"新文科"建设的时代愿景。开辟外语学科建设的全新思路，是当前外语教学改革的重要突破方向。

"中国科学院大学研究生教材系列"将切实满足特定专业学生群体的英语学习需求作为教材编写的重要依据，充分考虑到具体学习者群体的学习目标和学习诉求，具有以实际应用为导向的根本特质。该系列教材不仅关注教材编写前期的需求分析，同时重视教材试用阶段使用者的实际反馈，因为我们认为，直面使用者反馈是确定教材价值的关键一环，是重新审视学习者需求的宝贵机会，更是反复改进教材质量的可靠抓手。

"中国科学院大学研究生教材系列"融入现代信息技术，运用语料库的数据处理方法，整理归纳学科英语的语言特点和语篇特征。语料库方法可以十分客观快捷地捕捉学术语篇中的词汇、短语、搭配、语块、句子结构等语言层面的使用规律，正在成为学术和学科英语研究领域新近涌现的热点之一。然而，语料库技术运用于教材编写的尝试却寥寥无几，该系列教材无疑为语料库方法运用于教材编写做出了开创性的贡献。语料库的运用不仅能够呈现自然学术语境中真实的语言使用，更为重要的是，能够引导学习者建立适合自己微观研究方向的专业文献语料库，并将其作为未来学术生涯的开端以及追随学术生命成长过程的见证。学科英语语料库一方面可以成为研究者文献阅读经历不断累积的记录，另一方面也可能成为研究者写作不竭的灵感源泉和他们未来指导学生进行专业写作的宝贵财富。基于学科英语语料库的教材建设在"授人以鱼"的同时也在"授人以渔",而学习者也会因此获得"授人以渔"的能力。

我们正处在一个教育变革的时代。新的时代呼唤符合国家发展需求的教育理念和新颖实用的教学方法,同时也鼓励教师队伍努力探索新型的教材编写模式。"中国科学院大学研究生教材系列"积极响应时代的要求,是国家"新文科"建设指导思想下的勇敢尝试。

该系列教材的出版得到中国科学院大学教材出版中心资助,在此表示感谢。

高　原

2022 年 5 月

前　言

21世纪初，清华大学出版社曾出版过一本名为《英汉双语化学入门》的教材。该书曾入选教育部普通高等教育"十一五"国家级规划教材，是当时国内少有的着眼理工科专业英语的教科书。此书作者为已故中国科学院院士、南开大学化学系教授申泮文先生。他不仅以此教材为本科生开课，通过原汁原味的英语介绍化学专业基础知识，还在书中向读者传授了快速自学英语的方法。在当时的科学家群体中如此真诚关心学生英语学习之人实属罕见。

近年来，我国学者在国际科研舞台上扮演着日益重要的角色，而能否用英语在国际顶级学术期刊上发表论文无疑是衡量我国科研人员水准的主要依据之一。这就对我国科学专业领域的学习者和科研工作者的英文水平提出了更高的要求。拿化学专业来说，用英语撰写毕业论文并尽可能发表在国际期刊上已成为国内各大高校化学专业对研究生的基本要求。无论是为了应对眼前毕业需要还是为了谋求未来学术发展，英文专业论文写作能力的重要性不言而喻。

本教程旨在帮助化学专业的同仁更有效率地提高英文论文写作水平，在国际发表过程中少在语言问题上走弯路。

内容概览：

本教程共分为五章。第一章介绍如何自建专业语料库及其基本应用。第二章至第五章分别聚焦论文的 Introduction、Methods、Results 和 Discussion 部分，其中每章开头为 Corpus in Use 活动，引导学生利用自建专业语料库探索该章节所聚焦的论文部分的主要语言特点及难点；每章中间为一系列设计连贯的教学活动（Activity），用来操练各部分的写作重点；每章结尾按照写作逻辑和语言功能列出了该论文部分的常用功能语句（Functional Expressions and Sentences）。本教程还在附录部分为读者提供了常用化学词缀表（Appendix II Common Affixes in Chemistry）、常用化学缩略语和首字母缩写词表（Appendix III Common Chemical Abbreviations and Acronyms）以及一篇选自 *Nature Chemistry* 的示例论文

（Appendix IV Model Research Article）。全书活动练习配有答案（Appendix I Keys to Exercises）。

教程特色：

一、基于语料库编写。全书教学活动中所用的语言实例和常用功能语句均基于编者建立的化学专业语料库，利用语料库软件 AntConc 检索结果，辅以人工识别筛选而来。为了建立用于编写本书的语料库，编者收集了来自 JACS、Nature Chemistry、Inorganic Chemistry、ACS Catalysis、Analytical Chemistry 等国际期刊的论文共 280 篇，主要涉及无机化学（50 篇）、有机化学（50 篇）、物理化学（50 篇）、分析化学（50 篇）、高分子化学（50 篇）和其他专业方向（30 篇）。

二、授之以渔。本教程指导学习者自建化学专业语料库，并通过 Corpus in Use 活动帮助其练习使用语料库软件进行检索，传授学生自主探索本学科论文语言特点的方法。

三、精讲多练。本教程针对学生论文写作时的痛点和难点，设计了大量的教学活动（Activity），帮助学生高效、切实地提高论文写作能力。学生通常需要在活动中完成一个层层递进的学习过程，即"观察例文 → 理解逻辑 → 识别功能语句 → 练习功能语句用法 → 在语境中运用功能语句"。教学活动之间必要之处配有语言精练的讲解，既能帮助学习者进一步理解所学，也不会对非英语专业人士造成过大的阅读负担。全书的讲解部分均在灰色方框内，用斜体字呈现，例如：

> *The main purpose of the Introduction of a paper is to justify the research. ... so they can tell a better story based on the whole picture of the research. (See Page 9.)*

教程适用对象：

化学及相关专业研究生；化学方向学科英语教师。

本教程既可帮助学习者短时间内掌握化学英语论文写作的核心，也可作为论文写作的案头参考工具书，还向读者介绍了自建学科语料库的学习方法。希望这本教程能为读者的科研论文写作与发表助一臂之力。并且，和申泮文先生一样，编者也祝愿化学专业的朋友们都能学好英语。

杜　朋

2022 年 6 月

Contents

Chapter 1   **Building Your Own Corpus**   1

     1.1 What Is a Corpus?   2
     1.2 How to Build a Chemistry-specific Corpus   2
     1.3 What You Can Do with Your Own Corpus   4
     1.4 How to Create a Chemistry-specific Word List   5

Chapter 2   **Introduction**   7

     Corpus in Use   7
     Lead-in Questions   9
     2.1 A Story to Justify the Research   10
     2.2 Big Issue vs. Research Question   11
     2.3 Telling the Story   12
     2.4 Writing the Opening   14
     2.5 Writing the Funnel   16
     2.6 Writing the Aim   19
     Functional Expressions and Sentences   23
     Assignments   35

Chapter 3　　Methods　　37

Corpus in Use　　37
Lead-in Questions　　38
3.1 Purpose, Tense, and Voice　　39
3.2 Using Passive Voice in Methods　　41
3.3 Dealing with Experimental Details　　41
Functional Expressions and Sentences　　44
Assignments　　52

Chapter 4　　Results　　53

Corpus in Use　　53
Lead-in Questions　　54
4.1 Visual Illustrations　　56
4.2 Tables vs. Figures　　57
4.3 Presenting Results　　59
4.4 Subordinating Table and Figure Legends　　61
4.5 Subordinating Methods　　62
Functional Expressions and Sentences　　64
Assignments　　69

Chapter 5　　Discussion　　71

Corpus in Use　　71
Lead-in Questions　　72
5.1 Developing a Model　　73
5.2 Answering the Research Question　　74
5.3 Supporting the Answer with Results　　76
5.4 Relating Results to Previous Research　　77
5.5 Ending Discussion　　79
Functional Expressions and Sentences　　82
Assignments　　86

	References	87
	Appendixes	**89**
	Appendix I Keys to Exercises	89
	Appendix II Common Affixes in Chemistry	102
	Appendix III Common Chemical Abbreviations and Acronyms	107
	Appendix IV Model Research Article	118

Chapter 1
Building Your Own Corpus

1.1 What Is a Corpus?

A corpus is a principled collection of texts, written and/or spoken, which is stored on a computer (Biber et al., 1999). This collection of texts can be used for qualitative and quantitative analysis. This analysis can be carried out rapidly by using a computer.

There are several online corpora available, such as BNC (British National Corpus), BAWE (British Academic Written English), and COCA (Corpus of Contemporary American English). Learners of English can use them to improve their English by observing authentic language examples, which is more reliable than a speaker's intuition. For example, if you search for *lack* in BNC, you will get the following concordance.

much had nothing over, and he that gathered little had no	lack	; they gathered every man according to his e
New York Times saying: In looking at a painting today, " to	lack	a persuasive theory is to lack something cruc
because physical entities — such as neurons -	lack	certain qualities — such as intentionality or
this " homelessness " " anyway? Homelessness to me is a	lack	in any particular individual 's case of whateve
in do about our muscle type. The only way to minimise this	lack	is by yet further skill-acquisition. Yet no matte
tournament in every way, despite suffering from so many	lack	lustre performances from some of the leading
if an organism had a memory this bad it would ipso facto	lack	object permanence. Moreover, we know that
, the non-conserver is failing to exert central control (	lack	of " direction, inhibition, and co-ordination ")
em with a clicking heels bow. Despite his almost complete	lack	of English and the poor Italian the others pos
than a harsh, faceless drive for productivity. Even the	lack	of a catchy slogan at the decade 's end (" Th
pensions and living alone had a car. The combination of	lack	of access to a car, difficulty in using public tra
rope, Amnesty released a document outlining the apparent	lack	of accountability of the security forces. Death
me, as if he could not quite believe my laughter and my	lack	of agitation. I smiled at both of them and told
a part of what is important to me. I do not suffer from a	lack	of ambition, I simply accept life as it is. " Man

Figure 1.1

By observing this concordance, we can see that *of* should not be used after the verb *lack*. For students who study chemistry, however, a chemistry-specific corpus needs to be built to enable these students to learn language features in chemical research articles.

1.2 How to Build a Chemistry-specific Corpus

You can build this chemistry-specific corpus by collecting chemical research articles. To guarantee the size of this corpus, you are expected to collect at least 30 full articles from your target journals. It may be difficult for an individual to build such a large corpus, but this can be done by working together with your classmates. You and your classmates can build your chemistry-specific corpus and learn how to use it in the following steps.

Step 1: Form a group of six people who have the same or similar research direction, e.g. inorganic chemistry.

Step 2: For each group member, find five full research articles published in recent five years from your target journal, the journal where you want to publish your article, e.g. *Journal of the American Chemical Society*. These articles should have at least four sections, including Introduction, Methods, Results, and Discussion. If you do not have a target journal, you can ask your supervisor for help.

Step 3: Collect the text documents (.txt) of the five articles. You can follow these steps:

1. Visit the target journal website and access the full text of the article you want to collect.

2. Copy the text, paste it to "记事本" on your computer.

3. Omit tables, figures, acknowledgements, supplementary information, and references.

4. Save the file by section (Abstract, Introduction, Methods, Results, Discussion).

5. Put the saved files into different folders.

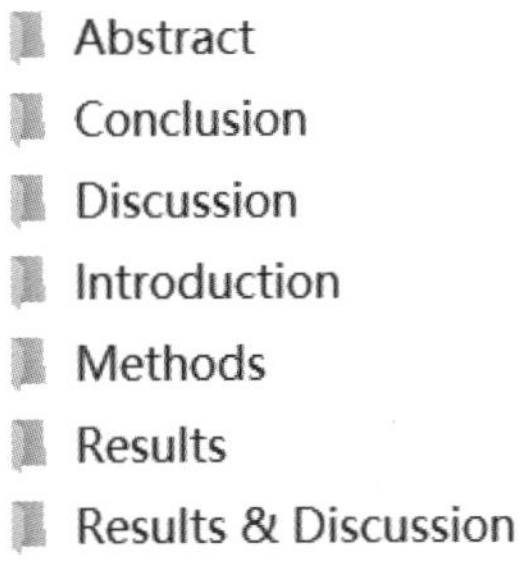

- Abstract
- Conclusion
- Discussion
- Introduction
- Methods
- Results
- Results & Discussion

Figure 1.2

6. Congratulations! You have built your chemistry-specific corpus.

Step 4: Download a corpus tool.

1. Search "AntConc Laurence Anthony" in your search engine. Visit the official website of AntConc.

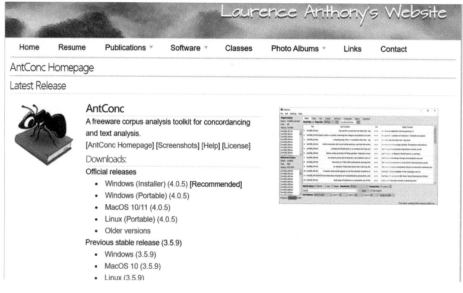

Figure 1.3

2. Download different versions of AntConc according to your computer system.

3. Click "Help" on the home page and learn the basic operation of AntConc. Use the corpus you just built for practice.

1.3 What You Can Do with Your Own Corpus

With you own chemistry-specific corpus, you will be able to investigate some interesting features of the language used in chemical research papers. For example, you can look at in what way the verbs *decrease* and *reduce* are used differently by using the "Concordance" function. You may get results like these.

```
              mainly used in conventional CCC to  decrease retention time for analytes with large
           only several milliseconds, and need to  decrease retraction velocity to reduce instability due
       erties. Fluorescence lifetimes and quantum yields  decrease significantly upon bromide substitution on the
                  and stress at constant strain both  decrease slightly after the first cycle, suggesting
              remedy or functional food to help  decrease stress and fatigue in health care [2,3].
        isplaying a considerably high crystallinity. This  decrease suggests that PC71BM has merged
    /z 202 and 216 show a disproportionately larger  decrease than the aliphatic ions (m/z 202
              brain parenchyma cells is promising to  decrease the Ab burden [28]. However, insufficient BACE1
          of H2O2 (100 μM) could remarkably  decrease the absorption of DPBF by 31%. Control
              lithium-ion cell are favorable to  decrease the battery internal resistance due to
              lithium-ion cell is favorable to  decrease the battery internal resistance due to
            over 60 h with almost no potential  decrease. The catalyst is ideally suited for
   lectron-withdrawing \xA8CCF3 group significantly  decrease the CTC formation through the steric
```

Figure 1.4

```
                        peak resolution as well as to reduce retention time [23\xA8C26]. Elution\xA8
  5 -SNAP doped PVDF tubingcan more effectively reduce risk of bacterial infections. Interestingly, com
              self-discharge should be minimized. To reduce self-discharge, it is appropriate to
                    , we report a new approach to reduce self-discharge of supercapacitor based on
        lower molecular weights were synthesized to reduce severe aggregation to study the relationship
        higher temperatures, however, their ROM rates reduce sharply as their TT-CM conversion
              SAPs showed that SAPs could effectively reduce shrinkage, cracking potential, and change the
        drug solubility, enhance therapeutic effect and reduce side effects [1], [2], [3], [4], [5], [6], [7], [
              3 perovskite, the(001) peak is observed to reduce, simultaneously, new peaks atcorresponding to (11
                        to be a simple method to reduce surface tension and to improve drop
  at intraventricular injection of Infliximab could reduce tau hyperphosphorylation significantly in APP/PS1
        inter-molecular interac- tions, which should reduce Tg [29,30]. PI-1, derived from the rigid
              3 groups can also be effective to reduce the absorptions at 1310 and 1550 nm.
                          of the PIs so as to reduce the absorptions of C\xA8CH
        be catalyzed.34, 35 Therefore, LTO may likewise reduce the activation energy of the sulfolane (
```

Figure 1.5

From these concordances, we can see that *decrease* is used both as an intransitive and transitive verb, while *reduce* is often used only as a transitive verb.

1.4 How to Create a Chemistry-specific Word List

To many first-year chemistry postgraduate students, it is difficult to read research papers because of the large number of unknown words. If you have a list of words that are frequently used in the papers of your research direction, then you will be able to learn these words extensively. This would greatly improve your reading speed and efficiency.

You can do this by using the "Word List" function of AntConc. Load your corpus and click "Word List" button, and then AntConc will generate a word list of your corpus by frequency.

Figure 1.6

Of course, there are lots of unwanted words in this word list, such as articles, prepositions, pronouns, auxiliary verbs and words you have already known. You can work with group members to select the words that are meaningful to you and create your own word list specific to your research direction.

Chapter 2
Introduction

↘ Corpus in Use

In addition to making a chemistry-specific word list, corpus tools can help us do many other things, especially in learning vocabulary. By searching a corpus, we can quickly find out how to use some confusable words by observing a large number of authentic language examples presented in the concordance. For example, *although* and *despite* are two words that often appear in the Introduction of a paper. Writers often use these two words to introduce an unsolved problem or to identify a knowledge gap. But these two words are used differently. Can you now find the difference by searching your own corpus and then complete the following tasks?

I. Combine these sentences using "*Although...,*" to form contrastive statements identifying knowledge gap.

1. Little research has been reported on the application of amide functionalized carbon supports.
   Many studies have reported the use of nitrogen doped carbon nanostructures.
   _____
   _____

2. Many researchers have designed novel endcapping agents to develop new imide resins.
   Few studies on the imide oligomers derived from fluorinated phenyethynyl-contained endcapping agents could be found in the literature.
   _____
   _____

3. The identification of novel, non-steroidal RORg antagonists for therapeutic use still remains an urgent need.
   Significant progress has been made in developing RORg antagonists.
   _____
   _____

II. Combine these sentences using "*Despite...,*" to form contrastive statements identifying knowledge gap.

1. There have been encouraging advances during the past few years.
   The NRR activity and selectivity are still far from satisfactory.
   _____
   _____

2. There has been no general and practical solution to allow for the use of amine bases in Pd-catalyzed C-N cross-coupling.
   Researchers have made considerable efforts.
   _____
   _____

3. We have achieved great progress in the development and optimization of triazolylidene carbenes as catalysts for enantioselective reactions.
   Fundamental studies of these species are relatively limited.

   _____

   _____

↳ Lead-in Questions

Despite other variations, many research papers adopt the following IMRD (Introduction, Methods, Results, and Discussion) structure. Work in pairs and discuss the following questions.

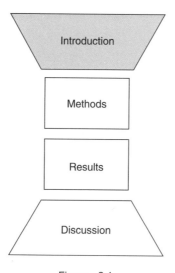

Figure 2.1

1. What is the purpose of an Introduction?

2. Why do you think in the above figure the Introduction section is drawn in that shape?

> The main purpose of the Introduction of a paper is to justify the research. Writing an Introduction is like telling a story of why you decided to do your research and why it is worth doing. Although Introduction is always the first section of a paper, writers often start to write this section after finishing Methods, Results, and Discussion, so they can tell a better story based on the whole picture of the research.

2.1 A Story to Justify the Research

● *Activity 1*

A. To justify your research, in the Introduction you need to tell readers the Known, Unknown, Question, and Approach. Match the description for each of them.

1. Known   a. Research aim, question, or hypothesis
2. Unknown   b. What is established or believed about the topic
3. Question   c. Ways to find out the answer to the question
4. Approach   d. Problems, knowledge gaps, possibilities

B. Read the following simplified Introduction. Identify the Known, Unknown, Question, and Approach.

① Steroids are a large family of physiologically and pharmaceutically important natural products. ② Previous studies toward the chemical synthesis of steroids have facilitated the development of steroid based drugs. ③ However, the additional biological functions of structurally unusual steroids, such as Aplysiasecosterol A (1), remain to be explored. ④ In this work, we aim to explore the biology of Aplysiasecosterol A by accomplishing the first and asymmetric total synthesis of (1) in a convergent fashion.

Source: Lu, Z., Zhang, X., Guo, Z., Chen, Y., Mu, T., & Li, A. (2018). Total Synthesis of Aplysiasecosterol A. *Journal of the American Chemical Society, 140*(29), 9211–9218.

1. **Known:**   Sentence(s) _____
2. **Unknown:**   Sentence(s) _____
3. **Question:**   Sentence(s) _____
4. **Approach:**   Sentence(s) _____

In the simplified Introduction, are there any words and expressions signaling the Known, Unknown, Question, and Approach? Underline them and then compare your answer with your partner.

C. Use some of the signal language you underlined in Exercise B to complete the following paragraph.

Recently, _____ have reported different kinds of strategies to achieve controllable generation of NO triggered by UV, vis, and even NIR light. _____, the poor tissue penetration of UV and vis as well as the low efficiency of NIR light significantly limits their effective applications. In this study, we _____ overcome these problems _____ introducing scintillating nanoparticles (SCNPs) as the energy transducers to convert the high-penetrating X-ray into UV-vis lights in situ, and further activate the surrounding photoactive donors to release NO.

Source: Du, Z., Zhang, X., Guo, Z., Xie, J., Dong, X., Zhu, S., Du, J., Gu, Z., & Zhao Y. (2018). X-Ray-controlled Generation of Peroxynitrite Based on Nanosized LiLuF4: Ce3+ Scintillators and Their Applications for Radiosensitization. *Advanced Materials*, *30*(43), e1804046.

Now look at the papers in your research field and highlight words and expressions signaling the Known, Unknown, Question, and Approach.

2.2 Big Issue vs. Research Question

In research papers, writers often tell a story about solving a problem. They tend to present this problem in the Introduction from general to specific. This means they need to identify the big issue that attracts attention in a certain research field and to state their own specific research question. It is important to understand the difference between the big issue and the research question.

● ***Activity 2***

For each of the following sentence pairs, identify the big issue (BI) and the research question (RQ).

1. a. How to develop a method for monitoring the biological HClO in living organisms.
   b. How to prepare a photostable and biocompatible fluorescent probes for accurate imaging of biological HClO in multiple living animals to assess the usefulness of this probe.
2. a. What are the chemical and biological functions of secosteroids, a subclass of steroids featuring a ring cleavage of the original tetracyclic framework?
   b. What are the additional functions of structurally unusual steroids?

3. a. How to accurately isolate and detect disease-specific exosomes.

   b. How to develop methods for direct exosome isolation and subsequent naked-eye, colorimetric, and electrochemical detection that avoid the use of a commercial "total exosome isolation kit"-based preisolation step commonly used in existing exosome-analysis methods.

2.3 Telling the Story

> *Readers may feel confused if they only know the big issue and the research question but have no idea where they come from. To make the story in the Introducton logical and easy to follow, writers also need to provide readers with more information, such as the background about the research topic, explanation of key terms, and the knowledge gap based on the Known and Unknown.*

• ***Activity 3***

Read the Introduction of a research paper and answer the questions.

Cancer, known as a life-threatening disease, causes millions of people to die every year due to its high metastatic diffusion capacity and fatality rate, and it significantly affects the human health and public safety. Early and accurate diagnosis of cancer, which may offer valuable information on enhancing the therapeutic efficiency and play a critical role in improving survival rate of cancer patients, is in great demand.

With the development of biological and medical techniques, tumor biomarkers appeared and served as important indices for risk assessment and early cancer detection. Unfortunately, traditional techniques, including X-ray, CT, and B ultrasound concentrating on morphological changes of tissues, cannot meet this demand, and they result in missing the best times for cancer therapy.

Given the problems above, considerable efforts have been devoted to developing novel biosensing techniques for cancer early diagnosis through identifying the abnormal expression of tumor biomarkers in biological samples. Among these techniques, the homogeneous electrochemical sensing strategy is regarded as an ideal tool due to its immobilization-free characteristic, which not only simplifies the operation procedure and lowers the detection cost but also avoids the steric hindrance effect to strengthen the recognition and response efficiency.

Chapter 2
Introduction

However, it is worth noting, that these reported homogeneous electrochemical techniques have several of the following drawbacks. First, most of the previously reported homogeneous electrochemical strategies suffered from the complicated and expensive signal molecule-participated labeling procedure, making the development of homogeneous electrochemical biosensors more difficult. Second, in order to improve the sensitivity, such developed biosensors depend on enzyme-assisted signal amplification strategies, which failed to achieve fast detection and would heighten the cost. Third, all the homogeneous electrochemical biosensors commit themselves to single tumor biomarker detection, easily resulting in false positive diagnosis because the expression level of tumor biomarkers can also be influenced by other factors (inflammation and infection).

For the sake of addressing the issues above and as a continuation of our studies, we attempt, here, to develop a label-free and enzyme-free homogeneous electrochemical strategy for ultrasensitive and simultaneous detection of multiple tumor biomarkers.

Source: Chang, J., Wang, X., Wang, J., Li, H., & Li, F. (2019). Nucleic Acid-functionalized Metal-organic Framework-based Homogeneous Electrochemical Biosensor for Simultaneous Detection of Multiple Tumor Biomarkers. *Analytical Chemistry, 91*, 3604 – 3610.

1. What is the general research topic?
   _____

2. What is the big issue of this study?
   _____

3. What is the knowledge gap?
   _____

4. How is information about the knowledge gap organized?
   _____

5. What is the research aim?
   _____

6. How does the research aim connect to the knowledge gap?
   _____

Now compare your answers with a partner and discuss what signal language may help you find out these answers quickly.

> *From Activity 3, we can see that an Introduction covers lots of information. This section therefore should be well-organized. A common organization of Introduction includes three major parts: Opening, Funnel, and Aim. In each part, writers focus on different purposes and tend to use signal language to indicate these purposes.*

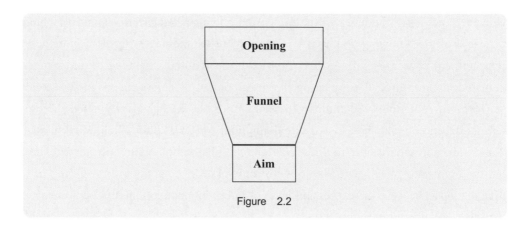

Figure 2.2

2.4 Writing the Opening

The opening part of an Introduction should engage and attract the reader's attention, so writers usually begin the Introduction with the significance of the research topic. They may also need to define and explain the key terms in this study and finally identify the big issue facing the research community.

● ***Activity 4***

A. Read the first two paragraphs of the Introduction in Activity 3 and look at the opening sentences in the following paper. Work in pairs and discuss the purpose of the opening part.

CO_2 is a major greenhouse gas, contributing to global warming and climate change. The largest source of CO_2 emissions is from the burning of fossil fuels for heat, electricity, and transportation. The EU has committed to cutting greenhouse gas emissions to 80% below 1990 levels by 2050. The process of capturing CO_2 is the most efficient abatement technique in terms of tons of CO_2 removed from the atmosphere; however, the subsequent carbon storage has significant shortcomings, including high investment costs, uncertainty of potential long-term storage capacity, and increased public resistance.

Source: Wang, L., Yi, Y., Guo, H., & Tu, X. (2018). Atmospheric Pressure and Room Temperature Synthesis of Methanol Through Plasma-catalytic Hydrogenation of CO_2. *ACS Catalysis*, *8*(1), 90–100.

Chapter 2
Introduction

B. Read the opening of the following paper and identify the significance, key term and big issue.

① Steroids are a large family of physiologically and pharmaceutically important natural products. ② They often serve as signaling molecules for activation of steroid hormone receptors. ③ Despite the progress achieved in this field, the additional biological functions of structurally unusual steroids remain to be explored.

Source: Lu, Z., Zhang, X., Guo, Z., Chen, Y., Mu, T., & Li, A. (2018). Total Synthesis of Aplysiasecosterol A. *Journal of the American Chemical Society, 140*(29), 9211–9218.

• *Activity 5*

A. In the opening part, writers often use different expressions to establish the significance of the research in several ways. Put the expressions below in the correct category.

vital for	a promising tool	of great importance	extensively studied
a powerful technology	key role	be studied for centuries	economically important
useful method	low-cost	enormous interest	economically friendly

　　Research interest: _____

　　Usefulness: _____

　　Economic reasons: _____

　　Importance: _____

B. Use some of the above expressions to complete the following sentences.

1. Metal iodates have been _____ in the 1970s by Bell Laboratories.
2. DAPK plays a(n) _____ in a wide variety of cell death signaling pathways.
3. Nanocarriers are considered to be _____ in the delivery of drugs and genes.
4. Optically active organoboron compounds are _____ in synthetic chemistry.
5. Planting concrete has been regarded as a(n) _____ alternative to traditional impervious concrete.
6. DMFCs have attracted _____ as a potential green power source used for multi-functional electronic devices and vehicles.

15

● **Activity 6**

A. Read the two texts in Activity 4 and write down the expressions signaling the big issue. Then read the papers you collected and see if you can find out more signal language for the big issue.

Text A:

Text B:

B. Use the words and expressions below to complete sentences.

however (×3)	although	despite	not…yet
remains unconquered	several limitations	a major problem	there is much room
remains challenging	rarely		

1. _____, _____ associated with sulfonated polyimides is their poor water stability.
2. _____ significant advances, _____ for improvement in efficiency, lifetime, and safety of metal and metal-ion batteries.
3. _____ the field of organic electronics has witnessed much progress in device performance during the past few years, _____ are holding back its further development.
4. _____, the largest challenge concerning the reliability of the catalyst _____.
5. Water-dispersed microcapsule formulations have _____ been industrialized _____ and even _____ reported.
6. _____, it _____ to develop therapeutic nanoparticles for brain diseases such as Alzheimer's disease.

2.5 Writing the Funnel

After the Opening, writers need to narrow the big issue down to the research aim or research question. This narrow-down part is often called the Funnel. In the Funnel, writers review previous studies, construct a knowledge gap, and justify their research question by referencing to literature, including published research articles, review articles, books in a given field, etc.

Chapter 2
Introduction

• **Activity 7**

A. Read the following Introduction and put the Funnel (a–d) into the right order.

Steroids are a large family of physiologically and pharmaceutically important natural products. They often serve as signaling molecules for activation of steroid hormone receptors. However, the additional biological functions of structurally unusual steroids remain to be explored.

a. In 2015, Kigoshi, Kita, and Kawamura reported the isolation of Aplysiasecosterol A from the sea hare Aplysia kurodai. This secosteroid possesses an unprecedented tricyclic γ-diketone core attached by a densely substituted cyclopentane moiety.

b. Studies toward the chemical synthesis of steroids have facilitated the development of steroid based drugs and the evolution of the strategies and methods for the construction of polycyclic molecules. In the past decade, the renaissance in this area resulted in a series of elegant syntheses of structurally and biologically interesting steroids, such as batrachotoxinin A, cephalostatins, cortistatins, cyclocitrinol, cyclopamine, dafachronic acid A, hydroxysarmentogenin, nakiterpiosin, and ouabagenin.

c. However, the biology of Aplysiasecosterol A has not been sufficiently explored, presumably due to its natural scarcity, posing a considerable challenge for a de novo synthesis.

d. In 2016, Sung, Sheu, Wu, and co-workers reported the isolation of pinnigorgiols A, B, D, and E (4−7) from the gorgonian Pinnigorgia sp., which share an Aplysiasecosterol A type scaffold and vary slightly in their side chains. Interestingly, 4 was found to induce apoptosis of hepatic stellate cells via the ROS−ERK/JNK−Caspase-3 signaling pathway.

Herein, we report the first asymmetric total synthesis of Aplysiasecosterol A.

Source: Lu, Z., Zhang, X., Guo, Z., Chen, Y., Mu, T., & Li, A. (2018). Total Synthesis of Aplysiasecosterol A. *Journal of the American Chemical Society*, *140*(29), 9211–9218.

B. Use the words and expressions below to compete the diagram.

Funnel	Specific Studies	Framing the Knowledge Gap
Overview of Previous Studies	Knowledge Gap	

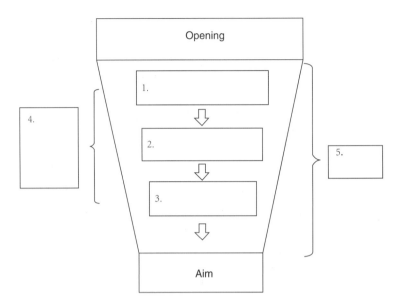

• Activity 8

A. Read the following paragraph and identify the signal language highlighting the knowledge gap.

The development of methods that generate enantioenriched N-alkylated indoles has been an active area of research for the past few years. The majority of these processes involve the enantioselective N-allylation of indoles with electron-withdrawing groups or with substituents blocking the C3 position. In addition, two-step procedures including N-allylation/oxidation of indolines and N-allylation/Fischer indolization of aryl hydrazines have been developed. Despite these notable advances, methods for highly enantioselective N-alkylation (nonallylic alkylation) of indoles with broad substrate scope remain rare. The difficulty in controlling regioselectivity in indole alkylation reactions originates from the nucleophilic character of the indole, with the C3 position being much more nucleophilic than N or other positions. We hypothesized that if the indole could be employed as an electrophile instead of as a nucleophile, alkylation reactions could potentially occur at positions other than C3.

Source: Dennis, J., White, N., Liu, R., & Buchwald, S. (2018). Palladium-catalyzed Carbon−nitrogen (C−N) Bond Formation Has Become a Valuable Tool in the Modern Synthesis of Structurally Complex Target Molecules. *Journal of the American Chemical Society, 140*(13), 4721–4725.

Read the papers you collected and find out more signal language of this kind.

B. A common way to highlight a knowledge gap is to use a negative subject to begin the sentence. This kind of subjects often include the following nouns: *research, study, work, investigation, attempt, information, researcher, attention*. Which of these nouns are countable and which are uncountable? Put the countable and uncountable nouns respectively into the correct box below.

However, few [ ] ...   However, little [ ] ...

C. Use the above two structures to revise the following sentences to highlight the gap.

1. X has been reported on the application of amide functionalized carbon supports.

_____

2. X are carried out directly using corrosive biofilm in the rust layer.

_____

3. X has been focused on the utilization of sulfone units in helicene synthesis.

_____

4. To our knowledge, X have been carried out on the correlation between the microstructure and gas separation performance of polyimide membranes.

_____

5. There are relatively X about the influence of anions on the crystal structures of L so far.

_____

2.6 Writing the Aim

> At the end of an Introduction is the Aim, where writers often state research aim, research question or hypothesis. For many chemistry papers, writers also briefly introduce the experimental approach in this part.

Activity 9

Read the following two texts and the text in Activity 8-A, and then identify the signal language highlighting the research aim, research question, hypothesis and experimental approach.

Consequently, the crucial boundaries between the physiology and pathology of BACE1 indicate that its expression must be precisely regulated, allowing the enzyme to perform its physiological functions while avoiding serious consequences of over-or under-expression. The BACE1 antisense (BACE1-AS) is a natural antisense transcript non-coding RNA that regulates BACE1 expression. The reduction of Ab by BACE1-AS knockdown with specific siRNA has been demonstrated previously via 14-day continuous pump-mediated infusion. Herein, we aim to achieve the BACE1-AS down-regulation through the less invasive intravenous administration by delivering the BACE1-AS shRNA encoding plasmids (pshBACE1-AS), which are more stable in circulation than siRNA.

Source: Liu, Y., An, S., Li, J., Kuang, Y., He, X., Guo, Y., Ma, H., Zhang, Y., Ji, Bin., & Jiang, C. (2016). Brain-targeted Co-delivery of Therapeutic Gene and Peptide by Multifunctional Nanoparticles in Alzheimer's Disease Mice. *Biomaterials*, *80*, 33–45.

With regard to chiroptical phenomena leading possibly to non-linear optics applications, circularly polarized luminescence (CPL) has been studied in the past and more recently, CPL exhibited by simple hexahelicenes, like carbo [6]-helicene, the shortest configurationally stable helicene at room temperature, however was rather weak, whereas other putative systems for non-linear optoelectronics, such as inherently chiral thiophene systems, were found to exhibit significant CPL both in monomeric, dimeric and higher-order oligomeric forms.

In this work, we wish to examine whether and to what extent the presence of hetero-atoms in the helicene backbone could promote a CPL response, since in previous work, the presence of a nitrogen atom in the hexahelicene backbone in position 2, leads to an increase in CPL.

Source: Abbate, S., Bazzini, C., Caronna, T., Fontana, F., Gangemi, F., Lebon, F, Longhi, G., Mele, A., & Natali Sora, I. (2007). Experimental and Calculated Circular Dichroism Spectra of Monoaza Helicenes. *Inorganica Chimica Acta*, *360*, 908–912.

Read the papers you collected and find out more signal language of this kind.

Activity 10

A. It is important to use specific language to signal the reader that you are stating the research aim, research question or hypothesis. Use the expressions in the box to rewrite the sentences below.

In this work, we examine…	Herein, we investigate…
The purpose of this study is to determine…	In this study we hypothesized that…

1. Is PhABCG1 involved in VOC emission?

   _____

   _____

2. What are the preferred pathways for CH_3OH formation from CO_2?

   _____

   _____

3. What types of Pd-Cu bimetallic alloy structures on the surface facilitate CO_2 hydrogenation to CH_3OH?

   _____

   _____

4. Both transmittance and reflectance spectra are probably appropriate for sensing experiments with these MCM structures.

   _____

   _____

B. Some other verbs are also used when stating a research aim. Use the verbs in the box to complete the sentences below.

report   identify   analyze   design   test   explore

1. The goal of this study was to _____ the active constituents of N. chinensis.
2. In this work, we decided to _____ the robustness of diradical 2 toward evaporation.
3. With these in mind, we aim to _____ an inorganic–organic hybrid lead-halide semiconductor.
4. Inspired by this, we are fascinated to _____ more interesting structures and properties of sulfonic ligand MOFs.

5. In this study, we _____ the successful application of structure-based virtual screening in novel RORg antagonist discovery.

6. The purpose of the present study is therefore to _____ the effect of applying urea modified multiwall carbon nanotubes as support for Pt nanoparticles.

- **Activity 11**

A. Match signal language for an experimental approach with its corresponding research aim, research question or hypothesis.

1. In this work, we question whether…   a. To test this hypothesis, we…

2. Herein, we investigate…   b. For this purpose, we…

3. The purpose of this study is to determine…   c. To answer this question, we…

4. In this study we hypothesized that…   d. For this investigation, we…

B. You can write a separate sentence to introduce the experimental approach after stating the research aim, research question or hypothesis. Match the questions and approaches below. Then use some of the signal language in A to write two cohesive sentences.

Questions	Approaches
What is the samples' effect on the resistance to carbon deposition and catalytic activity?	Used the simple solvent-swelling method.
Is it possible to impregnate a synthetically fluorinated NO donor into fluoropolymers?	Tested samples prepared with glycine, urea and without fuel.

1. _____

2. _____

C. You can also use linking words to combine the sentence stating the research question and the sentence introducing the experimental approach. These linking words include *by*, *using*, *by using*. Use them to respectively combine the two pairs of separate sentences you wrote in B into two signal sentences.

1. _____

2. _____

Chapter 2
Introduction

 Functional Expressions and Sentences

A. Establishing the significance of the general research topic

* X is vital for...
* X lays the foundation for...
* X is of great importance for...
* X has been widely investigated by...
* X has attracted extensive studies on...
* X may also play an important role in...
* X is fundamental to Y since it enables...
* X, which..., provides a promising tool for...
* X has received particular attention because...
* X is of significant importance. For example,...
* X is one of the most promising approaches to...
* X is the most powerful technology to analyze...
* X has demonstrated to be an excellent tool for...
* Understanding of X is of extreme importance for...
* Over the last decade, X has found applications in...
* X has received attention for its potential ability to...
* X is widely used in many industrial fields, such as...
* Because of..., X has attracted significant attention.
* X has been a well-known phenomenon for centuries.
* X is essential for many biological processes, such as...
* X as...is one of the most promising technologies to...
* X has been studied for centuries and it is now related to...
* For this reason, X has attracted enormous interest from...
* Accordingly, X is of great significance, which is helpful to...
* In the past decades, X has attracted great attentions owing to...
* X has been regarded as one of the most promising methods to...
* X could significantly improve the survival rate of patients with...
* X and its compounds are extensively used in different industries such as...
* X has attracted considerable interest across the scientific community for decades.
* X has received increasing attention as the promising...due to the advantages of...

* *A growing body of theoretical and experimental research is attempting to understand...*
* *X has attracted tremendous attention because of its crucial roles in various fields, such as...*
* *X differs significantly from Y due to..., which may find application in many areas, such as...*
* *X, which usually refers to..., is one of the most widely used strategies during the past decades.*
* *X has been extensively applied as...in many fields due to its attractive characteristics of...*
* *X has currently attracted enormous research interest because of its great promising use for a wide range including...*
* *In recent years, X has shown enormous progress primarily due to an emergence of...and the development of...*
* *X, which..., has emerged as one of the most promising strategies to solve serious environmental and energy problems.*

B. Identifying the big issue

* *X poses a serious threat to...*
* *X raises great concerns about...*
* *An important question related to...is...*
* *Up to now, it is still a great challenge to...*
* *However, the issue of...cannot be ignored.*
* *However, X poses a technical challenge for...*
* *X has caused severe...pollution, particularly in...*
* *X has become a serious environmental problem in...*
* *Therefore, X has been of a long-standing concern in...*
* *The lack of X remains a key barrier for the use of technology to...*
* *However, X is severely impeded because of its...(disadvantages)*
* *Although X is frequently used to..., Y often has adverse side effects.*
* *Nevertheless, X is...(disadvantages), which greatly restricts its application.*
* *However, only a small number of X can..., which restricts the application of Y in...*
* *X has become a critical environmental problem worldwide and is particularly apparent in...*
* *X, which has been widely used to prepare Y, is not preferred for environmental reasons currently.*
* *Although X might be effective to some degree, its widespread application is restricted because of...(disadvantages)*

C. Introducing recent research development in general

* *Early studies suggested...*
* *Up to date, studies have shown...*
* *Several studies have investigated...*
* *...experiments have revealed that...*
* *...materials have been explored for...*
* *...has been revealed by many studies.*
* *A line of studies has demonstrated that...*
* *Research efforts have largely focused on...*
* *Several strategies have been explored for...*
* *Tremendous efforts have been devoted to...*
* *In recent years, X has been regarded as an emerging...*
* *Various methods have been used to..., such as...*
* *X has so far been the dominating...reagents for...*
* *Recent research attempts focus on... For example,...*
* *Since the first report of X, ...has been explored for...*
* *Recently, X has emerged as promising materials for...*
* *...strategy has been originally coined and developed since...*
* *Various...systems have been exploited based on...to achieve...*
* *In particular, significant progress has been reported recently on...*
* *To date, a wide range of...applications have been demonstrated.*
* *In recent years, X has been identified as a promising approach to...*
* *Intensive research efforts have been made to design and synthesize...*
* *X is extensively studied due to the excellent properties. For example,...*
* *Since the discovery of X, a wide interest in the study of...has emerged.*
* *In the last 20 years, rapid development of X has provided effective ways to...*
* *Over the past 15 years, substantial progress has been made in understanding how...*
* *In the last few decades, considerable progress has been made in the development of X.*
* *Over the last few years, the design and application of... have achieved great successes.*
* *X has been developed over the last two decades for various applications ranging from...to...*
* *X, another effective strategy, ...(advantages) and thus has been widely utilized for Y in recent years.*
* *In recent years, considerable efforts have been devoted to X because of its wide applications in...*
* *Recently, considerable efforts have been invested/given to X because it exhibits unique*

properties, such as...
* *A study of the X therefore provides an opportunity to..., in addition to expanding our limited knowledge of...*

D. General reference to previous research: highlighting paucity of research

* *It still remains challenging to...*
* *However, this approach cannot...*
* *Despite..., it is unclear whether...*
* *To our knowledge, no studies have...*
* *However, how X relates to Y is unknown.*
* *However, X has largely been overlooked.*
* *In terms of...research, X remains unstudied.*
* *Hence, X has not been solved systematically.*
* *However, little attention has been focused on...*
* *However, until now, X remains poorly understood.*
* *By now, only a handful of studies have focused on...*
* *However, ...remains an unsolved challenge due to...*
* *At present, few...have been successively developed.*
* *X is still not clear as there are few studies in this area.*
* *Consequently, the development of X is in great demand.*
* *However, X suffers from significant limitations including...*
* *The intrinsic challenge of...makes it difficult to develop...*
* *Unfortunately, most of the involved systems are limited to...*
* *While X has been investigated, Y remains largely unexplored.*
* *However, X will lead to...and...will aggravate the problem.*
* *However, the mechanism of X has not yet been fully elucidated.*
* *However, this simplistic mechanism has recently been challenged.*
* *Multiple studies have demonstrated..., yet X remain to be explored.*
* *Although Diels–Alder reactions represent..., challenges in...do exist.*
* *However, the molecular mechanisms that...are incompletely understood.*
* *Currently, there are no specific methods to...and...could only rely on...*
* *However, X still remains a great challenge, limiting its practical application.*
* *One possibility to improve X is to..., which comes at a cost of...*
* *Owing to..., X possess poor..., therefore, leading to an unsatisfactory effect.*
* *Although..., the critical issue of... still encourages the community to advance...*
* *X, however, is not completely understood due to relatively few studies in this field.*

Chapter 2
Introduction

* However, to our knowledge, investigations in recent years have provided no data on...
* According to our understanding, to date successful use of X has not yet been published.
* Unfortunately, although X has been frequently reported, ...is hitherto scarcely known.
* Clearly, X causes a great challenge for the fabrication of...to achieve best performance.
* However, most of the previous studies only focused on..., and systematic studies on... are still scarce.
* While the fundamental chemistry of X is fairly well understood, there is surprisingly little information on Y.
* Although this method is an efficient strategy for..., it is inapplicable to...
* To date, X has received little attention.
* Despite..., X often remains a serious bottleneck for long-term measurements.
* Another major challenge is to...
* Some...systems have been developed to..., exhibiting remarkable effects, but it is inescapable to face the limitation of...
* Although X has been described extensively in a range of...globally, the literature describing the presence of X is limited.
* Even though X is now well established, few studies have successfully applied it to Y and there is currently no consistent way to Z.

E. Reporting findings of previous studies

* It was reported that...
* It was also found that...
* Most research to date has shown that...
* Previous studies have identified X...
* Previous studies have shown that...
* Plenty of evidence suggests that...
* Recent research has demonstrated that...
* Recent studies increasingly consider...
* Recent studies showed/reported that....
* Recent studies/investigations have shown that...
* Several studies describe...
* Some studies have shown that...
* Other studies have pointed out that...
* Some researchers have proposed that...
* The methods for...mainly include...
* The commonly used methods include...

* *The latest findings provide further evidence...*
* *The factors responsible for this change may include...*
* *Genome-wide transcriptomic studies have identified...*
* *Animal and human experiments have provided evidence for...*
* *Some recent theoretical models and mechanisms have been proposed to provide guide and reference for future development of...*

* *X is known to...*
* *X has been applied to...*
* *X was found to exhibit ...*
* *X was found...in our previous work.*
* *X is considered an important component of...*
* *X, which has been reported to have...effect on...*
* *X has become a popular and useful analytical tool in...*
* *X is capable of yielding a high level of...under...even with...*
* *X has previously been shown to have good potential to reduce...*
* *X has been shown to impact..., leading to increased incidence of...*
* *X was also found to..., although no structural detail has yet been reported.*
* *X has enabled...and paved the way toward commercially available devices.*

* *Previously, we reported...*
* *Previously, Thomson et al. (2013) demonstrated that X impairs...*
* *Recently, Thomson et al. (2013) reported that...*
* *Recently, scientists proposed a novel method to...*
* *Recently, ...was reported by Hou and co-workers.*
* *Recently, a small number of...have been studied due to...*
* *Recently, some investigators have demonstrated the application of...*
* *Recently, an alternative process for...was proposed and studied in detail.*
* *Recently, a novel approach for...was developed and high performance has been demonstrated.*
* *More recently it has been shown that...*
* *Very recently, ...has achieved a high PCE of...*
* *Very recently, ...has been reported by Thomson et al. (2013).*

* *In our previous works, we showed that...*
* *In subsequent studies, X was found to...*
* *In recent works, ...has been manifested by...*

* *In the past years, ...has been designed for...*
* *At present, the commonly used...materials are...*
* *Until now, various...have been constructed and showed enhanced activity.*
* *To improve the efficacy of X and reduce side effects, numerous strategies have been proposed in recent years, such as...*
* *In this context, several studies focused on..., with a wide variety of additives, have been published.*
* *The ingestion of X has shown to have negative effects on... from different environments in laboratory-based studies.*

* *Thomson et al. (2013) investigated...*
* *Thomson et al. (2013), using..., observed that...*
* *Thomson et al. (2013) reported the evidence of...*
* *Thomson et al. (2013) reported that..., particularly...*
* *Thomson et al. (2013) demonstrated for the first time that...*
* *Thomson and co-workers briefly reviewed the most relevant...studies on...*
* *...was revealed by Thomson et al. (2013).*
* *...has been reported by Thomson et al. (2013).*
* *One of the earliest...was reported by Thomson et al. (2013).*

F. Highlighting a knowledge gap in the research field or weaknesses of previous research

* *X shows a great challenge to...due to...*
* *X is not suitable for industrial production.*
* *A major disadvantage of this approach is...*
* *One problem is that... Another problem is that...*
* *In particular, it is extremely difficult to achieve...*
* *Overall, due to..., ...is still not entirely understood.*
* *So far, it is not possible to completely...in any...method.*
* *This strategy allows for..., but restrictions currently exist for...*
* *This means that a crucial link in understanding...is still to be established.*
* *Some serious disadvantages of X limit the development of Y, for instance, ...*
* *At the same time, the...problem in actual industrial production cannot be ignored.*
* *While extensively developed, X usually exhibits low levels of...and the scope of Y remains limited.*
* *Only X was reported for the...method, which needs further improvements to meet the requirements of practical applications.*

* *Although..., ...is difficult.*
* *Although..., it is constrained by...*
* *Although X represents..., it may not thoroughly predict...*
* *Although X has been frequently reported, Y was usually absent in the...*
* *Although this method is an efficient strategy for..., it is inapplicable to...*
* *Although all these methods are able to..., they commonly lack sensitivity for...*
* *Although this method allows for..., X still constitutes an analytical challenge for...*
* *Although the performance of X has been improved, there are still some drawbacks in..., for example, ..., which may limit the further efficiency improvements of...*
* *Even though..., few studies have successfully applied...and there is currently no consistent way to...*

* *However, one limitation of X is...*
* *However, ...has remained unclear.*
* *However, such a method is unable to...*
* *However, X remains a challenge, because of...*
* *However, the realization of...is still challenging.*
* *However, the details of X remain to be elucidated.*
* *However, its key problem for industrial application is...*
* *However, ..., making detection and analysis extremely challenging.*
* *However, as far as we know, no attempt has been made using this kind of X to...*
* *However, ...of using X has yet to be studied.*
* *However, X has some disadvantages such as..., leading to limitations in its widespread application and commercialization.*

* *Despite the importance of..., studies have rarely focused on...*
* *Despite the early success in..., ...limits its further application.*
* *Despite the above-mentioned pioneering work, X has not been evaluated systematically.*
* *In spite of numerous studies on X, surprisingly little is known about the effect of Y.*
* *Nevertheless, there remain several shortcomings:...*
* *Nevertheless, X is rarely studied because of lacking...*
* *Nevertheless, most of the reported reactions show low...*

* *To the best of our knowledge, X is yet to be reported.*
* *To the best of our knowledge, X has not been reported yet.*
* *To the best of our knowledge, the application of X has not been reported.*

G. Stating the research aim or research question

* *The aim of this study is to…*
* *…is also presented and discussed.*
* *We here report the development of…*
* *The effects of X were also investigated.*
* *As far as we are aware, this study focuses on…*
* *In addition to exploring…, we also investigated…*
* *In continuing our effort, here we report…by using…*
* *Here/Herein, we report/study/present/describe/evaluate/…*
* *The objectives of this study were to detect…and to discuss…*
* *The effects of several factors on…were evaluated in this study.*
* *Additionally, we aimed to highlight whether…, thus providing insights on…*
* *We aimed to study/explore/investigate/examine/evaluate/demonstrate/determine…*
* *The work presented here is part of a series of studies in which we aim to understand…*

* *In the present study, we investigated…*
* *In this work/study, we report/focus on…*
* *In this paper, further attempts were made to explore…*
* *In this study, we proposed a novel linkage strategy for…*
* *In this study, to attain a significant improvement in…, we…*
* *In this work we compare and contrast…, with a particular focus on…*
* *In this work we wish to examine whether and to what extent X could…*
* *Throughout this paper, X will be investigated and it will be discussed in view of…*

* *To address this issue, we performed…*
* *To verify our hypothesis, we aimed to…*
* *To explore X, therefore, herein we report…*
* *To mitigate these challenges, we have demonstrated…*
* *To overcome these drawbacks, X has been widely studied.*

* *Hence, there is an urgent need to develop…*
* *Therefore, this work studies… and aims to…*
* *Therefore, in this study, we primarily focused on…*
* *Therefore, in order to find out X, a new approach for…was proposed.*
* *Therefore, a comprehensive analysis that can detect X is urgently needed.*
* *Therefore, in this paper, X is studied in detail, by evaluating the main factors, and their*

possible interactions, in order to optimize it.

* *Thus, there is an utmost urgency to develop X that could compensate for the shortcomings of...*

H. Stating the research hypothesis

* *We thus hypothesized that...*
* *We therefore inferred that...*
* *Therefore, we hypothesize that...*
* *The effect of X may have an impact on...*
* *As a consequence, we can suppose that...*
* *Based on our previous results, we hypothesized that...*

I. Highlighting the significance and novelty of the research

* *Therefore, this work shed light on...*
* *Here we investigated for the first time...*
* *Our research opens a new strategy to...*
* *Thus, better understanding X will enable...*
* *This work may provide a new insight into...*
* *Our study is the first thorough investigation that...*
* *Thus, this work lays the foundation for understanding...*
* *Therefore, it would be of great significance to develop...*
* *This work provides a unique platform and resource for...*
* *More importantly, X would open a window to real applications.*
* *The findings in our study will provide valuable information for...*
* *This study not only provides a possible insight into..., but also paves the way for...*
* *The exploration of X may not only widen the scope of...but also provide a clearer understanding of...*
* *This work demonstrates the potential of organic materials in..., thus making way for the application of...*
* *Therefore, a new strategy of...within the physiological range would significantly expand the application areas.*

J. Summarizing the research design and methods

* *Here, we used X to...*
* *We used X as a novel tool to...*
* *We establish a methodology to...*

* *Also, we characterized X using...*
* *In this study, we generated X using...*
* *Specifically, we investigated X using...*
* *In this work, we propose a method to...*
* *In this work, we design and synthesize...*
* *Herein, we engineered a novel tool for...*
* *In the current work we have used X as Y to...*
* *To circumvent the..., X has been developed to...*
* *Herein, we fabricate X to increase the efficiency.*
* *Our X strategy first involved... Next, ... Finally, ...*
* *Here we report a(n)...approach enabled by the...to...*
* *On the basis of..., we developed a new method to...*
* *In this work, we designed and synthesized a novel...*
* *To overcome these bottlenecks of..., we designed X.*
* *Based on the above considerations, X was designed.*
* *The property of X was studied by a series of methods.*
* *Therefore, X would be an effective method to realize Y.*
* *We design a(n)...molecule for the robust synthesis of...to...*
* *Three different preparative approaches were developed.*
* *The analytical methods developed for X detection include...*
* *X has been designed for developing the ligand-gated channel.*
* *The chemical structure of X was characterized by...(instruments).*
* *X is adopted as a promising strategy for further development of...*
* *In this work, X was prepared via...method and Y was obtained by...*
* *In order to achieve..., X should be optimized to be...to prevent the...*
* *We monitored and characterized X by different techniques, including...*
* *Based on these considerations, in this work, we design and synthesize...*
* *A test compound of...was selected for detailed mechanistic investigation.*
* *We systematically compared...and we performed detailed comparison of...*
* *We focus on the development of a(n)...strategy for comprehensive...analysis.*
* *In this paper, we chose X as..., and integrated it into one molecule via...*
* *X was identified, and Y was evaluated via...based on the identified products.*
* *This paper presents an extended...model which takes into account the influence of...*
* *In this work, quantum chemical simulations and experiments are combined to establish...*
* *Herein, we will discuss...of X, summarize several methods for X formation and its future perspectives.*

* *We used a combination of...approaches to elucidate and determine the fundamental mechanisms...*
* *This manuscript presents a(n)... strategy that consists of three phases. The first phase is... The second phase is... The third phase is...*

Chapter 2
Introduction

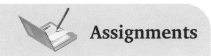

• *Reading*

Read the Introduction section of the article in Appendix IV. Try to find out the functional expressions and sentences according to the following model for Introduction.

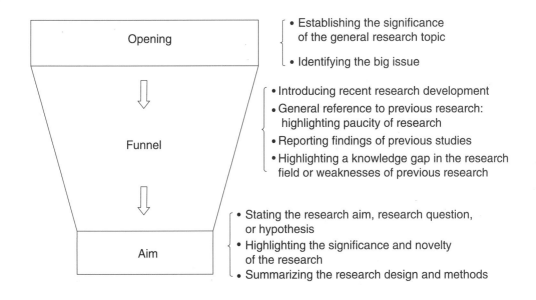

• *Writing*

Review what you learned in this chapter and use the above model to write an Introduction for your current or undergraduate research topic.

Chapter 3
Methods

↘ Corpus in Use

As we all know, prepositions are difficult for many English learners. A large number of prepositions will be used when describing chemical reaction conditions, such as temperature, concentration, air pressure and experimental instruments in the Methods section of a paper. To solve this problem, you can explore the use of common prepositions such as *in*, *at*, *by*, *with* and *to* in the Methods section by investigating in your own corpus.

Investigate your corpus and fill in the blanks with appropriate prepositions.

1. As shown _____ Figure 4, a bright image was observed _____ the red channel.
2. In the case of the hydrated sodium ion in perchlorate solution, the main peak is observed _____ 2544 cm\xA8C1.
3. However, these polysodium ions have never been observed _____ aqueous solution.
4. As discussed _____ Section 3.5.1, Pd-Cu (0.50) still consists of phases other than the dominant Pd-Cu alloy phase.
5. As has been demonstrated _____ previous studies, organic polymer materials have advantages over inorganic substrates.
6. As can be seen _____ a comparison of the two tables, peak oxygen uptake and exercise capacity are reliable predictors of quality of life.
7. It was coupled _____ a bundle of 8 400 \xA6\xCCm-core optical fibers as an excitation source.
8. All measurements were performed _____ room temperature.
9. Adsorption energies were calculated _____ \xA6\xA4E.
10. The number density of the particles was calculated _____ the total amount of gold used for the synthesis.
11. The detection limit that was then calculated _____ the following equation.
12. The emission signal was collected _____ the same objective and analyzed _____ an Acton spectrometer equipped _____ a liquid helium cooled CCD.

↘ Lead-in Questions

Although Methods is not the first section in a research paper, writers often choose to write this section earlier than the other sections when preparing their manuscripts. Work in pairs and discuss the following questions.

1. Why do writers often write Methods first?
2. What is the purpose of Methods?

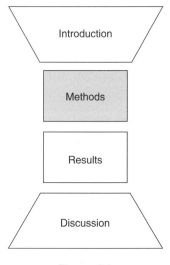

Figure 3.1

Chapter 3
Methods

3.1 Purpose, Tense, and Voice

In many chemical journals the Methods section is also called Experimental Section, Materials and Methods, or Computational and Experimental Methods. Some chemical journals require the writer to present information about Methods in a section called Supplementary Information.

The main purpose of this section is to tell the reader what researchers did to answer the research question and justify what they did. For a chemical research paper, in particular, the writer also needs to provide enough experimental details. Another thing that should be aware of is the tense and voice commonly used in this section.

• Activity 1

A. These sentences are from the Methods section of a research article "Changes in the Chemistry of Groundwater in the Chalk of the London Basin". First, put them into the correct order. Then, match the functions (a–i) with the nine sentences.

1. A total of 18 samples was collected and then analyzed for the isotopes mentioned earlier.
2. The samples were subsequently shipped to ISF for analysis by accelerator mass spectrometry (AMS).
3. The sites were selected from the London Basin area, which is located in the southeast of England and has been frequently used to interpret groundwater evolution.
4. Samples 1–9 were collected in thoroughly-rinsed 25 ml brown glass bottles which were filled to the top and then sealed tightly to prevent contamination.
5. The current investigation involved sampling and analyzing six sites to measure changes in groundwater chemistry.
6. Samples 10–18 were prepared in our laboratory using a revised version of the precipitation method established by the ISF Institute in Germany.
7. All tubing used was stainless steel, and although two samples were at risk of CFC contamination as a result of brief contact with plastic, variation among samples was negligible.
8. The filled bottles were shipped directly to two separate laboratories at Reading University, where they were analyzed using standard methods suitably miniaturized to handle small quantities of water.
9. This method obtains a precipitate through the addition of $BaCl_2.2H_2O$; the resulting

precipitate can be washed and stored easily.

a. The writer provides background information and justification.
b. The writer provides details about what was done and shows that care was taken.
c. The writer describes what was done by referring to existing methods in the literature.
d. The writer provides more details of the method.
e. The writer offers a general overview of this section.
f. The writer provides an overview of the procedure/method itself.
g. The writer continues to describe what was done in detail, using language which communicates that care was taken.
h. The writer provides more detailed information about the method and shows that it has been a good choice.
i. The writer mentions a possible difficulty.

B. Read this Methods section and see what tense and voice are mainly used. Work in pairs and discuss why this tense and voice are mainly used. Are there any other tenses being used? Why?

The current investigation involved sampling and analyzing six sites to measure changes in ground water chemistry. The sites were selected from the London Basin area, which is located in the southeast of England and has been frequently used to interpret groundwater evolution.

A total of 18 samples was collected and then analyzed for the isotopes mentioned earlier. Samples 1–9 were collected in thoroughly-rinsed 25 ml brown glass bottles which were filled to the top and then sealed tightly to prevent contamination. The filled bottles were shipped directly to two separate laboratories at Reading University, where they were analyzed using standard methods miniaturized to handle small quantities of water. Samples 10–18 were prepared in our laboratory using a revised version of the precipitation method established by the ISF Institute in Germany. This method obtains a precipitate through the addition of $BaCl_2.2H_2O$; the resulting precipitate can be washed and stored easily. The samples were subsequently shipped to ISF for analysis by accelerator mass spectrometry (AMS). All tubing used was stainless steel, and although two samples were at risk of CFO contamination as a result of brief contact with plastic, variation among samples was negligible.

Source: Glasman-Deal, H. (2009). *Science Research Writing for Non-native Speakers of English*. London: Imperial College Press, pp 58–66.

Chapter 3
Methods

 3.2 Using Passive Voice in Methods

> Passive voice is often used when people care more about the event (what happened) instead of the agent (who made the event happened). When reading a Methods section, readers pay more attention to the event (what the researchers did) rather than the agent (who the researchers are), so passive voice is often used to describe the procedure or methods. For example, a total of 18 samples were collected and then analyzed for the isotopes mentioned earlier.

● *Activity 2*

Rewrite the sentences below by using passive voice so that they focus on the underlined part.

1. I recorded <u>the electrical signals</u>.

2. The researchers fixed <u>the frequency of the power supply</u>.

3. We carried out <u>plasma hydrogenation of CO_2</u>.

4. The experiment measured <u>the change of the gas volume before and after the reaction</u>.

5. To evaluate the reaction performance of CO_2 hydrogenation to methanol, we calculated <u>the concentration of major products in the condensate</u>.

 3.3 Dealing with Experimental Details

> When writing Methods, writers need to provide sufficient details about their experimental procedure or research design, including what they did, materials (size, color, weight), instruments (appearance and function), reaction conditions (temperature, pressure, concentration), etc. This shows the credibility of their research and gives enough information for other researchers to repeat the research.

> However, texts with overwhelming details are difficult to read. You should select those important details relevant to the success of the methods and write about them in a concise way. The following sentence pattern is commonly used.
>
> | What was done + | Linking words + | Details |
> |---|---|---|
> | The signals were recorded | using/by using | a four-channel digital oscilloscope. |
>
> When writing this part, it is also important to describe the experimental procedure clearly and indicate that appropriate care was taken during the experimental operation.

● Activity 3

Use the following words and expressions to complete sentences providing sufficient details about methods.

1. carry out, plasma hydrogenation of CO_2, using, different DBD reactors, atmospheric pressure, at

   _____

2. feed into, the DBD reactor, a mixture of H_2 and CO_2, at a total flow rate of 40 ml/min

   _____

3. the discharge power, calculate, 10 W, the Q-U Lissajous method, by using, fix, at, in this work, and

   _____

4. the gaseous products, analyze, a gas chromatograph, equipped with, a thermal conductivity detector (TCD) and a flame ionized detector (FID), using

   _____

● Activity 4

To describe experimental procedure clearly, sequence expressions are often used. Complete the sentences below with the sequence expressions in the box.

after	first step	prior to	when	at the end of	subsequently	next

1. _____ testing, the test solution was purged with high-purity N_2.
2. The samples were _____ diluted 10-fold to get a 50% acetonitrile solution.
3. _____ being stirred at 80°C for 5 h, the solution was concentrated.

4. The _____ day, the cells were incubated with AP21998 at 25°C for 80 minutes.

5. _____ a positive voltage was swept across the device, a steady increase in current was observed.

6. The _____ was to make the graphite electrode as a substrate for Pt catalyst electrodeposition.

7. _____ the reaction, the reactor was cooled to room temperature.

• **Activity 5**

Chemical experiments require careful operations. Use the words and expressions in the box to complete the sentences indicating that appropriate care was taken during the experimental procedure.

tightly	slowly	under identical conditions	carefully
every	to prevent	three times	quickly

1. Cells were washed with DPBS for _____.
2. The hot solution was poured _____ into 100 ml of water.
3. Finally, the samples were _____ placed on the plate.
4. Then the membrane was taken out, _____ wiped with a tissue paper and weighed on a micro-balance.
5. The bottle was also _____ covered by a parafilm tape _____ the evaporation of water.
6. These tubes were kept _____ at room temperature and weighed _____ three days for 30 days.

Functional Expressions and Sentences

A. Restating research purpose and providing a general introduction of this section

* To reveal X, Y was employed as…
* To study X / the effect of X…, Y was performed in…
* To synthesize X, we carried out…
* To verify the impact of X, we applied…
* To investigate whether…, this study was done using…
* With the aim of gaining insights into X, various mathematical models including…were employed.

B. Giving the source of materials or equipment used

* X was supplied by…
* X was provided by Tianjin Fuyu Fine Chemical Co., Ltd.
* X was obtained from Sigma-Aldrich (St. Louis, MO, USA).
* X was purchased from Beijing Bomi Chemicals Corp., China.
* X was sourced from a local supplier with the water absorption capacity of…
* The genes of all the other enzymes were synthesized from Gene Universal.

C. Providing an overview of the materials or methods

* All calculations were based on…
* Gradient programming was used to perform…
* All measurements were performed at room temperature.
* X was characterized by a comprehensive set of techniques.
* All reagents were of analytical grade and all solutions were prepared with distilled water.
* All regents and chemicals are obtained commercially and used without further purification.
* All chemicals used were of analytical grade and used as received without further purification.

Chapter 3
Methods

D. Describing experimental procedure: typical subjects + verbs in passive forms

* The mixture was	*poured into...* *extracted with...* *reacted for 12 h at 80 °C.* *stirred at 100 °C for 24 h.* *concentrated under vacuum.* *allowed to react for 3 h at 75 °C.* *centrifuged at 700 rpm for 5 min.* *centrifuged and washed by...twice.* *heated to 100 °C / under reflux at 100 °C.* *cooled to room temperature and stirred for 3 h.* *filtered through...and the filtrate was evaporated...*
* The solution was	*poured into...* *transferred to...* *dried with/via...* *heated to reflux.* *passed through a(n)...* *concentrated to give...* *cooled to 50 °C.* *stirred at 100 °C for 12 h.* *diluted with.../to 500 ml by...* *cooled down to room temperature.*
* The samples were	*exposed to...* *rinsed with...* *stained with...* *dissolved in...* *washed with...* *evaluated by...* *transferred to...* *imaged using...* *analyzed with...* *incubated with...* *fabricated with...* *characterized by...* *prepared with/in...* *irradiated with.../twice for 5s.* *heated from 100°C to 200°C.* *outgassed at 80 °C for 12 h.*

45

* The reaction was	completed. monitored by… worked up by… quenched by/with… carried out by/in/at… stirred at room temperature for 5 h. kept at 200°C / at 500 Pa / under…atmosphere for 12 h.
* The residue was * The resulting residue was	dried in… purified by… dissolved in… dispersed in… extracted with…
* The cells were	seeded in… fixed with… rinsed with… stained with… washed with… transfected with… assembled using… cultured with/in… harvested after 24 h. observed under/by… incubated for/with/at…

E. Describing experimental procedure: sequence expressions

* The first step was to…
* In the first step, X was…
* During the second step, …
* To achieve X, we first prepared…
* The resultant mixture was first stirred at the same temperature for 30 min and then cooled to…

* Prior to a test, the catalysts were reduced by…
* Prior to testing, the specimens were sanitized using…

Chapter 3
Methods

* *Prior to analysis, all dried samples were derivatized using…*
* *Prior to experiments, the exposed surfaces of samples were…*

* *Next, a layer of unlabeled polymer was…*
* *The next day, the cells were incubated with…*
* *The residue was used in the next step without purification.*
* *In the next step, …was filtered and properly washed with ethanol.*

* *X was then added to the mixture.*
* *Then a certain amount of Li was deposited.*
* *The resultant mixture was then stirred at the same temperature for 0.5 h.*
* *The samples were then rinsed with deionized water, …, and subsequently…*

* *The resultant mixture was subsequently extruded 20 times.*
* *Thermodynamic parameters were subsequently calculated with the formula…*
* *The samples were subsequently diluted 10-fold to get a 50% acetonitrile solution.*
* *Subsequently, the solution was dialyzed against deionized water for 24 h.*

* *After 15 min / 12–14 days / 24 h / 10 cycles, …*
* *After cooled to ambient temperature, X was…*
* *After removal of the culture medium, X was…*
* *After the reaction, the mixture was poured into…*
* *After that, the cells were washed three times with…*
* *After sonication for…min, the aqueous solutions…*
* *After cooling to room temperature, the solution was…*
* *After washing three times with the culture medium, X was…*
* *After stirring at room temperature for 24 h, the mixture was…*
* *After cultured overnight / for 24 h, the medium was replaced by…*
* *After being stirred at 80°C for 24 h, the solution was concentrated.*
* *After the reaction was completed, the reaction mixture was cooled to 37°C.*
* *After incubation for 24 h in culture dishes, HeLa cells were washed with PBS and then treated with…*
* *After that, the solution was cooled down to room temperature, and then X was slowly added with agitation.*

* *Once the solution became homogeneous, X was added.*

* Once the solutions filtered, the solvent was evaporated and...
* Once the addition was complete, the reaction was monitored by...
* Once synthesized, the polymer was transformed into radical forms via...
* Once the mean tumor volume reached approximately 125 mm^3, the mice were divided into four groups stochastically.

* When these polymer solutions were exposed to UV irradiation, ...
* When the absorption peaks of H_2O were no longer observed, O_3 was introduced...
* When a positive voltage was swept across the device, a steady increase in current was observed.
* When the tumor volume had reached approximately 90 mm^3, the mice were randomly divided into the following six groups at day 0 and then received different treatments.

* Finally, the samples were carefully placed on the plate.
* Finally, the cell cycle distribution was analyzed by flow cytometry.
* At the end of the aging period, they were cooled to room temperature.
* Crystal decay was monitored by...at the end of data collection.
* Their final weight and dimension were measured for density, shrinkage, and porosity.

F. Describing experimental procedure: infinitive of purposes

* In order to investigate..., ...
* In order to estimate X, Y was...
* In order to remove X..., Y was...
* In order to minimize the effect of X, Y was...
* In order to calculate X, the following formula is used.

* To avoid..., ...
* To check..., ...
* To obtain..., ...
* To control..., ...
* To remove..., ...
* To prepare..., ...
* To calculate..., ...
* To determine..., ...
* To quantify X, we...
* To verify X, Y was...
* To compare X and Y, ...

* *To evaluate the effects of..., ...*
* *To achieve a correct condition, ...*
* *To ensure the accuracy of the results, ...*
* *To further analyze/explain/investigate..., ...*
* *To investigate X / the effect of X / whether..., ...*
* *To ensure overall neutrality of the system, ...*
* *To ensure the stability of the measurement, ...*
* *To achieve fair comparison among all samples, ...*
* *To fabricate electrochromic film substrates for SERS tests, ...*
* *To increase the range/stability/solubility/wettability of..., ...*
* *To prevent decomposition, the product was stored under...*
* *To prevent possible crevice corrosion, the specimens were treated using the following procedures.*
* *To accurately estimate X in a computationally efficient manner, 3D coordinates were generated for...*
* *To analyze..., the Bitplane (Concord, MA, USA) Imaris 3D/4D image processing and analysis software (version 8.4) was used.*

G. Describing experimental procedure: using/by/via + instrument/method

* *The slices were cut using a Diatome diamond knife.*
* *Using an alternative indirect method, we investigated...*
* *Analytical NMR spectra were recorded using a Bruker Avance III spectrometer.*

* *Cloud point curve was determined by a titration method at 25 \xA1\xF0C.*
* *By controlling the temperature and eliminating O_2 from the system, biomass fuel...*
* *The initial concentration of dissolved oxygen in the media was measured by a dissolved oxygen meter.*

* *Phase purity of all samples was confirmed via X-ray diffraction.*
* *The solution was dried via reduced-pressure distillation to obtain dry precipitation.*
* *Electrical connection to the electrode was made via an Au wire covered in parafilm to prevent exposure to electrolyte.*

H. Justifying choices made about methods

* *A preliminary test of X confirmed...*
* *This demonstrates the necessity of...*

* These procedures were selected because...
* The porous nature of X was confirmed with...
* X shows the expected mass increase after reduction...
* X was tested using the water vacuum saturation method.
* Although this method may..., our measurements indicate that...
* This choice does not affect the interpretation of the results because...

I. Indicating that appropriate care was taken

* All samples was analyzed in triplicate.
* To avoid..., ...was carried out for 15 min in the dark.
* All these procedures were performed in a N_2 atmosphere.
* Samples were cured for 30 days followed by drying at 75°C for 2 h.
* To evaluate reproducibility, each fermentation was carried out three times.
* These tubes were kept under identical conditions at room temperature and weighed every three 3 days for 30 days.
* The dried samples were carefully stuck onto X with Y and were sputter-coated with Z to make the sample conductive before testing.

J. Relating materials or methods to previous studies

* X has been described in our previous studies.
* The calculation was based on Flory's equilibrium theory, where...
* Using analogous methods to our previous work, X was introduced...
* The synthesis of X was done according to the procedure of Smith (1973).
* X mutations were carried out according to the PCR-based strategy using...
* X was prepared according to the procedure used by Smith et al. (2003).
* X was prepared according to the methods reported by Wang et al. (1998).
* According to previous reports by Wang et al., X was prepared using the following methods.
* The experimental procedure was carried out according to Smith et al. (2001) with some modifications.

K. Indicating where problems occurred

* X gave poor reactivity due to the lack of...
* Although..., X still results in problematic limited solubility.
* In addition, external mass transfer limitations are confirmed by...
* As there is a lack of major databases for process design related to X, ...

* *X cannot be measured due to the limitation of measurement technique.*
* *The substrate is not represented explicitly in the simulations, which may slightly reduce the overall red shift compared to the experimental results.*
* *Although an orthorhombic cell was assigned by the data collection program, satisfactory solution could not be obtained with orthorhombic space groups.*

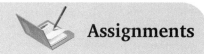# Assignments

- **Reading**

Read the Methods section of the article in Appendix IV. Try to find out the functional expressions and sentences according to the following model for Methods.

• Restating research purpose and providing a general introduction of this section • Giving the source of materials or equipment used
• Providing an overview of the materials or methods • Describing experimental procedure in detail • Justifying choices made about methods • Indicating that appropriate care was taken
• Relating materials or methods to previous studies
• Indicating where problems occurred

- **Writing**

Review what you learned in this chapter and use the above model to write a Methods for your current or undergraduate research topic.

Chapter 4
Results

↘ Corpus in Use

The main purpose of a Results section is to report the research findings. Therefore, reporting verbs are often used in this section. Common reporting verbs include *show, report, suggest, indicate, demonstrate, present*, etc. Is it possible for us to find out the most frequently used reporting verbs in Results? You can realize this by using corpus tools. Please use the Word List function of AntConc to seek the top ten verbs in Results according to your corpus. Compare the results with groups of other research directions, and see if there are any differences. Then use the Concordance function to observe how to use these verbs.

I. Use your corpus to find out the top ten frequently used verbs in Results.

1. _____
2. _____
3. _____
4. _____
5. _____

6. _____
7. _____
8. _____
9. _____
10. _____

II. With the help of your corpus, decide whether each verb in the table can be followed by a noun (noun structure), a *that*-clause, or both.

Verbs in Results section	Noun (noun structure)	*that*-clause
observe		
show		
use		
obtain		
find		
report		
calculate		
compare		
prepare		
determine		

↘ Lead-in Questions

Work in pairs and discuss what the following picture implies.

Chapter 4
Results

Figure 4.1

In a Results section, writers often use visual illustrations to help readers understand the results better. Common visual illustrations include line graphs, bar graphs, pie charts, tables, diagrams, and maps. In most chemical research papers, tables and figures are often used as visual illustrations and they are crucial to successful publication of a paper.

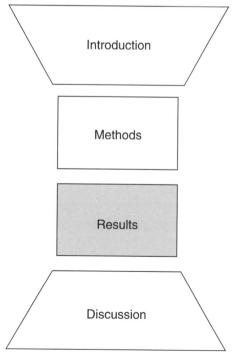

Figure 4.2

4.1 Visual Illustrations

● *Activity 1*

There are six examples of common visual illustrations used in academic texts. Complete the table below with the use of (a–f) and the example (A–F) of each type.

Uses: a. location   b. comparison   c. proportion

d. steps in a process   e. changes by time   f. statistical display

Types	Uses	Example
diagram		
table		
map		
pie chart		
bar graph		
line graph		

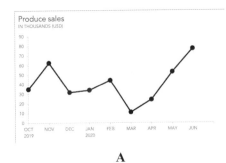

A

B

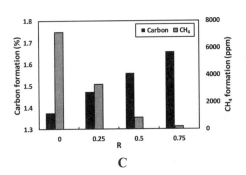

C

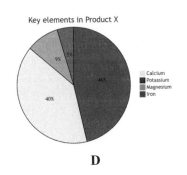

D

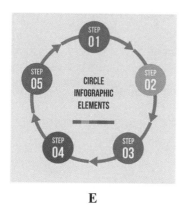

E   F

 ## 4.2 Tables vs. Figures

> For chemical papers, using good tables and figures as visual illustrations is critical. Tables are the arrangements of numbers and descriptions in rows and columns. They are often used for quantitative data. Figures, on the other hand, are usually graphs like line graphs, bar graphs and pie charts. They are often used for visualizing a trend of your data or the comparison between different sets of data. A table has a title, also known as a legend, telling the reader what the table is showing. Unlike tables, a figure legend is longer, containing a title and a caption. A caption should be a few sentences about what you need to know to interpret the data shown in the figure.

• ***Activity 2***

A. Look at the following table and figure. What differences can you see?

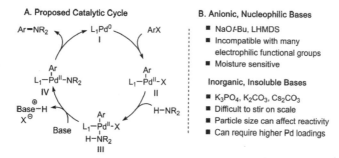

Figure 1. (A) The proposed catalytic cycle for the palladium-catalyzed coupling of aryl halides with amines: **I**, monoligated Pd(0); **II**, oxidative addition (OA) complex; **III**, amine-bound OA complex; **IV**, amido complex. (B) Synthetic considerations for bases employed in C−N coupling.

Table 1. Comparison of Ligands in Pd-Catalyzed Amination Facilitated by DBU[a]

precatalyst	nucleophile	temp (°C)	time	yield (%)
P1	aniline	RT	20 min	0
P2	aniline	RT	20 min	30
P3	aniline	RT	20 min	0
P4	aniline	RT	20 min	61
P5	aniline	RT	20 min	99
P6	aniline	RT	20 min	99
COD(L6-Pd)$_2$	aniline	RT	3 h	99
COD(L6-Pd)$_2$	benzamide	RT	16 h	76
COD(L6-Pd)$_2$	benzamide	60	16 h	97
COD(L6-Pd)$_2$	benzyl amine	60	16 h	98

L1, R = Cy, XPhos
L2, R = t-Bu, t-BuXPhos
L3, R = Cy, BrettPhos
L4, R = t-Bu, t-BuBrettPhos
L5, R = Ad, AdBrettPhos
L6, R = Ad, AlPhos
L7, R = t-Bu, t-BuAlPhos
L8, R = Cy, CyAlPhos

[a]Reaction conditions: aryl triflate (0.25 mmol), nucleophile (0.30 mmol), DBU (0.50 mmol), precatalyst (1% Pd; 2.5 μmol or 1.25 μmol dimer), MTBE (0.25 mL). GC and ^{1}H NMR yields referenced to hexamethylbenzene as an internal standard. MTBE = methyl tert-butyl ether.

Source: Dennis, J., White, N., Liu, R., & Buchwald, S. (2018). Palladium-catalyzed Carbon−Nitrogen (C−N) Bond Formation Has Become a Valuable Tool in the Modern Synthesis of Structurally Complex Target Molecules. *Journal of the American Chemical Society, 140*(13), 4721–4725.

B. You can present data by either tables or figures. Look at the following table and figure showing the same set of data. Which one do you think should be used in the paper?

Station	\multicolumn{5}{c}{ECOLOGICAL GROUP}
	I	II	III	IV	V
75U	91.3	5.3	3.2	0.2	0.0
75R	89.8	6.1	3.6	0.5	0.0
200R	69.3	14.2	8.6	6.8	1.1
500R	63.0	29.5	3.4	4.2	0.0
1000R	86.7	8.5	4.5	0.2	0.0

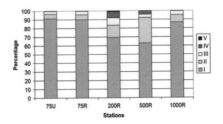

Source: Borja, A. (2014, June 24). 11 Steps to Structuring a Science Paper Editor Will Take Seriously. Elsevier website.

Chapter 4
Results

4.3 Presenting Results

Your experiment may generate a large quantity of data. Do you need to include all these experimental data in your paper? Are these data the results of your study? How do you decide whether the results should be presented or not? Before answering these questions, you need to understand the difference among data, results, and implication.

• Activity 3

A. Match the terms with their correct descriptions and examples.

Terms	Descriptions
Data	a. General statements that interpret data
Results	b. Thoughts, hypotheses, and speculation about what the results may mean for the big issue you identified
Implication	c. Facts obtained from experiments and observations

Examples

Example 1	+2.30, +3.46, +3.52 and +3.27 kcal/mol
Example 2	Our results suggest that a selection pathway based on energy-dissipative cycling could have driven the selective synthesis of phospholipids on early Earth.
Example 3	Propranolol given during normal ventilation decreased phospholipid concentration.

B. Work in pairs and discuss which of the following elements can be included in a Results section. Then tick your choices.

☐ Data

☐ Results that don't fit hypothesis

☐ Results not related to the research question

☐ Implications

☐ Research aim

☐ Statistical analysis

☐ Experimental results

C. Now work in a group and discuss how to decide what to present and not to present in a Results section.

• *Activity 4*

A. Organize the common steps of table and figure descriptions (a–d) according to the following paragraph.

① Experiments utilizing p-tolyl-OA complexes (Figure 1) as catalysts (1.0 mol %) to couple p-tolyl triflate with aniline revealed that multiple ligands are capable of facilitating the desired reaction (Table 1). ② Precatalyst P6 bearing L6 (AlPhos) and P5 (AdBrettPhos) provided nearly quantitative cross-coupling product at room temperature. ③ P4 (t-BuBrettPhos) provided the desired product in moderate yields and ligands bearing cyclohexyl (Cy) groups on the phosphine, including P3 (BrettPhos) and L1 (XPhos), failed to yield any of the desired product. ④ While P5 is highly reactive, the ligand from which it is derived is known to undergo an in situ ligand modification in the presence of aryl halides, generating different active catalytic species for each ArX substrate.

Source: Dennis, J., White, N., Liu, R., & Buchwald, S. (2018). Palladium-catalyzed Carbon−Nitrogen (C−N) Bond Formation Has Become a Valuable Tool in the Modern Synthesis of Structurally Complex Target Molecules. *Journal of the American Chemical Society, 140*(13), 4721–4725.

a. Choose only those results that answer your research question

b. Write a topic sentence stating the results and locating the table or figure

c. Analyze the data in the table or figure and interpret the results

d. Select data from the table or figure to support the topic sentence

B. According to the above organization you worked out, put the following sentences into the correct order.

1. Substrates bearing acidic functional groups, such as an unprotected pyrazole, an indole, and a phenol, are also compatible with the weakly basic reaction conditions when an excess of base is used.

Chapter 4
Results

2. To explore the scope of the methodology, a variety of aryl halides, triflates, and nucleophiles were tested (Table 2).

3. Both five- and six-membered heterocyclic amines, including a pyrazine, a thiazole, and an oxazole were coupled in high yield under the optimized reaction conditions.

Source: Dennis, J., White, N., Liu, R., & Buchwald, S. (2018). Palladium-catalyzed Carbon−Nitrogen (C−N) Bond Formation Has Become a Valuable Tool in the Modern Synthesis of Structurally Complex Target Molecules. *Journal of the American Chemical Society, 140*(13), 4721– 4725.

4.4 Subordinating Table and Figure Legends

Tables and figures are used to illustrate results, so writers need to locate tables and figures in their papers. For example,

Our experimental results are shown in Figure 2. Interestingly, both catalysts exhibit higher CH_3OH selectivity upon H_2O addition at a comparable level of CO_2 conversion.

In Results, however, we should emphasize the results interpreted from data rather than the tables and figures themselves. It is more powerful to write a sentence about results as the topic sentence than to write a sentence only about table or figure legends. Therefore, we can subordinate table and figure legends by citing them in parentheses after writing a result statement. For example,

Interestingly, both catalysts exhibit higher CH_3OH selectivity upon H_2O addition at a comparable level of CO_2 conversion (Figure 2).

● **Activity 5**

Revise the following sentences by using parentheses to subordinate table and figure legends.

1. Figure 1 shows the size distribution of GNPs. The size distribution has an average size of 60 \xA1\xC0 9 nm together with a typical TEM image as an inset.

   _____

   _____

2. Factors influencing the crystal habit are shown in Figure 2. The crystal habit is clearly reflected on the crystal structure of the solids.

   _____

3. The results of our experiment are presented in Table 3. Clearly, the alloy formation could considerably decrease the crystallite size of the Cu phase.

4.5 Subordinating Methods

In a Results section, writer may also write about methods to remind readers. However, it would be strange to write a separate sentence about methods in Results, where the focus should be results. There are several ways to subordinate methods in a Results section.

● **Activity 6**

A. Methods subordinated as subject: Revise the sentences below and make methods as the subject of the revised sentence.

E.g. We used DAPC analysis to examine mice during the acute and chronic phase. This analysis revealed a clear distinction between healthy and infected individuals during the acute and chronic phases (Figure 5).

↓

DAPC analysis of mice revealed a clear distinction between healthy and infected individuals during the acute and chronic phases (Figure 5).

1. H_2O_2 was added to convert GSH into GSSG. A significant fluorescence enhancement was observed (Figure 1).

2. An electrochemical testing was carried out. Chemical states of CoP/NCNHP catalyst are nearly not changed.

B. Methods subordinated in transition phrase: Revise these following sentences and put methods in a transition phrase.

E.g. We used DAPC analysis to examine mice during the acute and chronic phase. This analysis revealed a clear distinction between healthy and infected individuals during the acute and chronic phases (Figure 5).

↓

After DAPC analysis of mice, we identified a clear distinction between healthy and infected individuals during the acute and chronic phases (Figure 5).

1. H_2O_2 was added to convert GSH into GSSG. A significant fluorescence enhancement was observed (Figure 1).

2. An electrochemical testing was carried out. Chemical states of CoP/NCNHP catalyst are nearly not changed.

C. Methods subordinated in transition clause: Revise these following sentences and put methods in a transition clause.

E.g. We used DAPC analysis to examine mice during the acute and chronic phase. This analysis revealed a clear distinction between healthy and infected individuals during the acute and chronic phases (Figure 5).

↓

When DAPC analysis of mice was used, we identified a clear distinction between healthy and infected individuals during the acute and chronic phases (Figure 5).

1. H_2O_2 was added to convert GSH into GSSG. A significant fluorescence enhancement was observed (Figure 1).

2. We completed a desired catalytic reaction. Magnetic stir bars can then be easily separated from the reaction mixture.

Functional Expressions and Sentences

A. Reference to aim, research questions or methods

* For this purpose, we...
* We next investigated...
* To study the origin of X, we...
* We measured...to investigate...
* X was employed to investigate...
* X was carried out to investigate...
* We next tested X conditions on...
* To assess..., X was performed.
* X was demonstrated by analysis of...
* To assess the performance of X, we...
* To broadly examine..., we analyzed...
* To better resolve..., X was performed.
* Therefore, our efforts were focused on...
* To exclude that..., X was treated with...
* To begin, we tested the performance of...
* X is further probed via Y measurements.
* Since..., we sought to determine whether...
* In this work, we overcame...challenge by...
* The purpose of this study was to determine...
* To estimate/study..., we display...in Figure 1.
* To gain further insight into..., we performed...
* To enable the systematic study of..., we first...
* To obtain more information about..., we used...
* For the measurements of..., X was performed.
* To test if X is applicable to Y, we first examined...
* To assess the impact of X, Y was determined by...
* To elucidate..., we have determined...by (method).
* To investigate/evaluate/assess/explore/examine..., we...
* To further investigate the effect of X on Y, we synthesized Z.
* To demonstrate the utility of X process, we incorporated Y into Z.

Chapter 4
Results

* *X is generated with a common fabrication technique used for...*
* *In order to obtain X, parameters such as...were optimized when...*
* *To gain insight into the structural details and morphology of A, we...*
* *To figure out X, ...was brought into operation, as displayed in Figure 1.*
* *To delineate/investigate/evaluate..., we used/turned to...(instrument or method)*
* *To assess X, Y is investigated through molecular simulation using Gaussian program package and the density functional theory (DFT).*

B. Locating data in a table or figure

* *Table/Figure 1 shows...*
* *As shown in Table/Figure 1, ...*
* *...are evaluated/shown in Table/Figure 1.*
* *The results of...are listed in Table/Figure1.*
* *It can be seen from Table/Figure 1 that...*
* *The result is represented in Table/Figure 1.*
* *As depicted in Table/Figure 1, X shows..., indicating...*
* *Further analyses of...are provided in Table/Figure 1.*
* *The key parameters...are summarized in Table/Figure 1.*
* *Table/Figure 1 presents/depicts/provides/indicates...*
* *The data in Table/Figure 1 are unambiguous evidence that...*
* *To understand..., ...experiments were carried out in Table/Figure 1.*
* *As shown in Table/Figure 1, the concentration decreased from... to...*
* *As presented/depicted/provided/indicated in Table/Figure 1, ...*
* *As summarized in Table/Figure 1, this method displayed X in the range of...*
* *The currents across each membrane stack were increasing...(Table/Figure 1).*
* *We were able to identify X, the thicknesses of which are summarized in Table/Figure 1.*
* *To investigate..., ...were performed, and...were pleasing when optimizing the synthesis conditions (Table/Figure 1).*

C. Statements of positive results

* *This suggests that...*
* *As expected, we observed...*
* *These observations confirm that...*
* *We observed the production of X.*
* *X showed dramatically increased...*
* *This demonstrates that X increased...*

* Meanwhile, X showed an increase in...
* However, the latter results reveal that...
* This is consistent with the results from...
* This result further confirms the viability of...
* These data prove that X results in Y without Z.
* Consequently, it was observed that X exhibited...
* These results (Figure 1) confirm..., suggesting...
* With the success in..., we took a step further to...
* As expected, X was the most significantly enhanced by...
* The cell yields..., which are comparable to previous results.
* To some extent, it indicated that X would be increased with Y.
* When compared to X, a greater Y was observed in Z (Figure 1).
* In comparison to X, the appearance of Y confirms the successful...
* The above results all illustrated that X was successfully deposited onto...
* This value is in excellent agreement with..., confirming the possibility of...

D. Statements of negative results

* No product was detected in...
* Notably, X was not found to...
* X showed negligible Y production.
* Unfortunately, X is not sufficient to...
* However, when..., no X was observed.
* Contrary to our expectations, X did not...
* It is unclear why X was not detected with...
* However, for..., X did not perform as well as Y.
* These experiments yielded no apparent benefit of...
* X does not exhibit in this range, which indicates that...
* Although we were able to confirm..., we did not observe...
* In addition, we find that X does not seem to perform well in Y.
* However, when we..., the acquisition failed 2 of 3 times due to...
* Although previous efforts have demonstrated..., ...has not been reported.
* In the experimental range studied, the other factors and their interactions do not present a significant effect on...

E. Reporting a reaction

* We formed X with Y.

* *X was treated with Y at...temperature.*
* *After soaking in..., X was then placed into...*
* *To test X, Y was beveled into two parts to...*
* *X synthesized in this study was prepared by using...*
* *Moreover, a blank experiment was also conducted to understand...*
* *In the synthesis, while X was deliberately selected as..., Y was used as...respectively (Scheme 1).*
* *In this study, in addition to X in the Introduction section, another stepwise reaction is employed to...*

F. Highlighting significant, interesting or surprising results

* *Notably, ...*
* *It should be noted that...*
* *It is worth noticing that...*
* *Interestingly, X revealed that...*
* *Interestingly, X was observed to...*
* *Surprisingly, the results revealed that...*
* *Unlike X, Y emerged as two different signals.*
* *A particular advantage of X described here is...*
* *X indicated excellent reproducibility (Figure 1).*
* *However, our sample exhibited an unusual trend on...*
* *Impressively, ..., which is the highest recorded value for...*
* *There is a significant correlation between X and Y (Figure 1).*
* *To the best of our knowledge, X is the top value reported so far for...*
* *As shown in Figure 1, there were significant differences between X and Y.*
* *The results demonstrated that both X and Y were essential for Z, and further explained that...*
* *Compared to..., X increased, which significantly improved Y (see in Supplementary Figure 1).*
* *The obtained X exhibited excellent film forming property, and Y gave colorless, transparent and flexible films (Figure 1).*
* *It is rather unusual to observe X in..., unless it is somehow influenced by some external or internal driving forces, such as...*

G. Summary of the results

* *We could conclude that...*

* Hence, we conclude that...
* These results indicated that...
* These results suggested that...
* These results further demonstrate...
* Therefore, it can be concluded that...
* The above results demonstrate that...
* Together, these results demonstrate...
* This study essentially demonstrates...
* Taken together, our results imply that...
* There is thus a pressing need to identify...
* The experiments revealed/confirmed that...
* This study shows that X plays a vital role in...
* To this end, we summed up...and compared...
* In summary, we successfully demonstrated that...
* Taken together, our results provide important insights into...
* To sum up, the mechanisms of X may be summarized as follows.
* Due to its excellent selective..., X shows encouraging potential for...
* Therefore, the significant increase observed in X could be justified as...
* These results offer high probability of greatly improved X once Y is studied.
* These results demonstrated that..., thereby indicating that...
* Thus, it can be surmised that...
* Three reasons can be discussed to explain this phenomenon.
* Although X was demonstrated in this study, our method is expected to be applicable for...

Chapter 4
Results

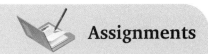
Assignments

- **Reading**

    Read the Results of the article in Appendix IV. Try to find out the functional expressions and sentences according to the following model for Results.

• Reference to aim, research questions or methods
• Describing data in a table or figure   ♦ Locating data in a table or figure   ♦ Highlighting significant data in a table or figure
• Reporting and commenting results   ♦ Statements of positive results   ♦ Statements of negative results   ♦ Reporting a reaction   ♦ Highlighting significant, interesting or surprising results
• Summary of the results

- **Writing**

    Review what you learned in this chapter and use the above model to write a Results section for your current or undergraduate research topic.

Chapter 5
Discussion

↘ Corpus in Use

In Discussion, writers often look at the large picture of the research field. When doing this, they tend to adopt a tentative tone rather than an absolutely certain attitude. They also try to show different levels of certainty when writing about implications, speculations, applications and recommendations. For these purposes, modal verbs like *may*, *might*, *would*, *could* and *should* are often used. How to use these modal verbs accurately is always challenging to English learners. Please use your corpus to investigate these words and learn how to appropriately use them in Discussion by observing the concordance. Then try to do the following exercise.

Investigate your corpus and see how frequently the following modal verbs are used in Discussion.

Modal verbs	Frequency
may	
might	
would	
could	
should	
must	

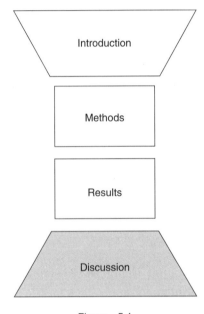

Figure 5.1

Lead-in Questions

The main purposes of Discussion are to answer the research question, explain how results support that answer and explain how the answer is related to previous research. Work in pairs and discuss the following questions.

1. How does the information in the Results section of a paper differ from the Discussion section?

2. Some papers include a Conclusion section. What is the difference between Discussion and Conclusion?

Chapter 5
Discussion

5.1 Developing a Model

> *The Discussion of a paper is to state the answer to the research question, support the answer with key results, and interpret the meaning of these results. You should also relate your findings to previous research and relate your research to the big issue addressed at the beginning of Introduction.*

• *Activity 1*

The Discussion below is from a research paper aiming to investigate the development of a biomimetic model complex of [Fe]-hydrogenase that incorporates a Mn, as opposed to a Fe, metal center. Read this section and use the expressions below to complete the model for Discussion.

Discussion

The active sites of both the semi-synthetic [Mn]- and [Fe]-hydrogenase lack the GMP moiety and two methyl groups in the pyridinol group of the native cofactor (Fig. 1a), which should be the principle reason for their specific activity being only a few percent of that of native [Fe]-hydrogenase. Direct comparison of the semi-synthetic [Mn]- and [Fe]-hydrogenases, however, reveals the relative catalytic competency of the two different metals. The occupancy-normalized specific activity of [Mn]-hydrogenase is 25% higher than that in the analogous [Fe]-hydrogenase for the forward reaction (3 U mg^{-1} at a 50% active site occupancy), which is the physiological reaction during methanogenesis. Thus, Mn appears to be more active than Fe for enzymatic H$_2$ activation.

In summary, a Mn(i) model of the active site of [Fe]-hydrogenase that is capable of splitting H$_2$ and catalyzing hydrogenation reactions has been prepared. Reconstitution of the apoenzyme of [Fe]-hydrogenase with this Mn(i) model leads to a [Mn]-hydrogenase, which is active for the [Fe]-hydrogenase reactions. These findings demonstrate the catalytic functionality of a non-native metal in a hydrogenase enzyme. The molar activity of this semi-synthetic [Mn]-hydrogenase is higher than that of its Fe analogue, which raises an intriguing question—why does nature choose Fe over Mn?

Source: Pan, H. J., Huang, G., Wodrich, M. D., Tirani, F. F., Ataka, K., Shima, S., & Hu, X. (2019). A Catalytically Active [Mn]-hydrogenase Incorporating a Non-native Metal Cofactor. *Nature Chemistry*, *11*(7), 669–675.

Interpreting the results
Relating to the big issue
Answering the research question
Re-summarizing the results in general
Supporting the answer with results

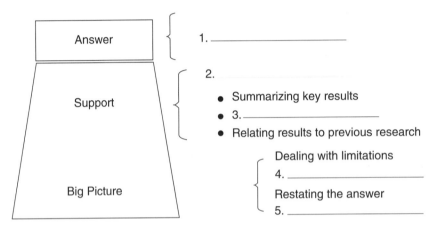

5.2 Answering the Research Question

> At the beginning of Discussion, try to answer the research question exactly as it was asked at the end of Introduction, using the same key terms, the same verbs if possible, and the same perspective. This can build good cohesion and coherence in your writing and thus help the reader follow your logic easily. For example, if the research question is "Does sympathetic stimulation increase norepinephrine synthesis in rat superior cervical ganglia in vivo?" The answer can be written as either "This study shows that sympathetic stimulation increases norepinephrine synthesis in rat superior cervical ganglia in vivo." or "This study shows that sympathetic stimulation does not increase norepinephrine synthesis in rat superior cervical ganglia in vivo."

- **Activity 2**

A. Use the following signal language to answer the research question exactly as it was asked.

This study shows that
Our results indicate that
In this study, we found that

Chapter 5
Discussion

In this study, we have shown that
In this study, we provide evidence that

Research Question (Aim, Hypothesis):

1. In this work, we examine whether PhABCG1 is involved in VOC emission.

   _____
   _____

2. The purpose of this study is to examine whether Mn addition promotes the formation of olefins.

   _____
   _____

3. In this study we hypothesized that both transmittance and reflectance spectra are appropriate for sensing experiments with these MCM structures.

   _____
   _____

B. Based on the research question and the result(s), use the signal language in A to write an answer to begin the Discussion.

Research Question (Aim):

> The purpose of this study is to investigate whether exposing oilseed rape seeds to neonicotinoids affects reproductive potential in wild bee populations.

Result(s):

> In wild bees, the number of queens was 24% lower after neonicitinoid treatment compared to the control ($P = 0.01$, explained variance = 59%) …

Answer (Discussion):

_____
_____

75

5.3 Supporting the Answer with Results

After answering the research question at the beginning of Discussion, you need to use relevant results as support to convince the reader that the answer is valid. However, do not simply repeat the result already given in the Results section.

• Activity 3

A. Read the result given in the Results section and the result presented in the Discussion section. What are the differences?

Result (Results):

> In wild bees, the number of queens was 24% lower after neonicitinoid treatment compared to the control (P = 0.01, explained variance = 59%) …

Result (Discussion):

> Neonicotinoid treatment decreased the number of queens in wild bee populations. Sublethal amount of neonicotinoids may have harmful effects on the reproduction of wild bees.

B. Use the following two transition phrases to connect the Answer (Discussion) and Result (Discussion) in A.

In our experiments, …   We found that…

Answer (Discussion):

> This study shows that exposing oilseed rape seeds to neonicotinoids affects reproductive potential in wild bee populations.

_____

_____

C. Use the following signal language to interpret the result in the box.

This result indicates that….   This finding indicates that…

This change/increase/decrease implies that… These findings suggest that…

This (summary of result) suggests…

> We found that neonicotinoid treatment decreased the number of queens in wild bee populations.

_____

_____

D. Use the transition phrases and signal language you learned in B and C to summarize and interpret the following result (Results).

> Of all of the environmental variables examined, pH showed the highest correlation with the bacterial community composition (r ¼ 0.677, P < 0.001), while adding the other factors did not improve the correlation (Table 3).

_____

_____

5.4 Relating Results to Previous Research

• Activity 4

A. Read the following texts and identify whether the results confirm, expand or contradict previous research results. What signal language indicates the relation between the results in present studies and in previous research?

1. The obtained results broaden the existing knowledge about the methane pathway of hydrocarbons formation from…
2. These findings show that…, which is again consistent with prior work by Chaffin et al.
3. This is in stark contrast to previous observations in carbonyl–olefin ring-opening metathesis reactions in which…

Try to find more signal language of this kind in the papers you collected.

B. Use the signal language in the box to complete the sentences below.

good agreement with	contradict	expand	comparable to

1. The obtained values are _____ recent studies also using SPR.
2. These results _____ previous reports which correlated higher hydrogen turnover frequencies.
3. These values are in _____ those reported by Ruprecht et al.
4. Our findings _____ the scope of prior work.

C. Based on the following information, write a paragraph that summarizes your result (Discussion), interprets that result, and relates it to previous research. Use the signal language and transition phrases you learned in previous activities.

Result (Results)

Of all of the environmental variables examined, pH showed the highest correlation with the bacterial community composition (r ¼ 0.677, P < 0.001), while adding the other factors did not improve the correlation.

Previous Research

Snow et al., 2012: pH showed no significant correlation with bacterial community composition.

Porter et al., 2017: pH was used to successfully predict bacterial community composition.

Chapter 5
Discussion

5.5 Ending Discussion

> When ending a Discussion section, as a reminder to the reader, writers may summarize the key results again and restate the answer to the research question. Then they often relate their research to the big issue identified at the Opening.
>
> The end of Discussion should be powerful and provide a take-home message for the reader, highlighting the contribution of your research to the science community. This can be done by stating implications, speculations, applications or recommendations.

● *Activity 5*

Read the following paragraph and identify which sentences summarize results in general, restate the answer, and relate to the big issue.

① In summary, a Mn(i) model of the active site of [Fe]-hydrogenase that is capable of splitting H_2 and catalyzing hydrogenation reactions has been prepared. ② Reconstitution of the apoenzyme of [Fe]-hydrogenase with this Mn(i) model leads to a [Mn]-hydrogenase, which is active for the [Fe]-hydrogenase reactions. ③ These findings demonstrate the catalytic functionality of a non-native metal in a hydrogenase enzyme. ④ The molar activity of this semi-synthetic [Mn]-hydrogenase is higher than that of its Fe analogue, which raises an intriguing question—why does nature choose Fe over Mn?

Source: Pan, H. J., Huang, G., Wodrich, M. D., Tirani, F. F., Ataka, K., Shima, S., & Hu, X. (2019). A Catalytically Active [Mn]-hydrogenase Incorporating a Non-native Metal Cofactor. *Nature Chemistry*, *11*(7), 669–675.

1. Summarizing results in general: _____

2. Restating the answer: _____

3. Relating to the big issue: _____

Activity 6

A. Match the terms with the descriptions.

1. Implication   a. Statement of advice based on results
2. Speculation   b. A possible future effect or result of answer
3. Application   c. Uses to which answers can be put
4. Recommendation   d. A logical guess that follows from an answer

B. For each of the following statements, identify whether it is an implication, speculation, recommendation, or application. What signal language indicates an implication, speculation, recommendation, or application?

1. The results imply that a uniform size hydrophilic domain (or clusters) does(do) not form in the hydrated polyimide ionomers.

2. Future work here should explore the potential to apply regional-TECs calculated from one section to sections from other animals.

3. The results here point to this design strategy as one that might be applicable to a wide range of emerging electrochemical applications.

4. We can reasonably speculate that the gold on the surface of the catalysts played a key role in the dissociation of hydrogen.

Try to find more signal language of this kind in the papers you collected.

C. Writers use different modal verbs to show different levels of certainty when stating an implication, speculation, recommendation, or application. According to the following information, complete the sentences.

Most Certain	application	(none)	can, will
	recommendation	recommend	should
	implication	suggest/imply	may, might
Least Certain	speculation	speculate	may, might

1. Our findings in mice, together with findings from studies of human coronary arteries, _____ (implication) that H1 blockers _____ _____ (antagonize)

Chapter 5
Discussion

histamine-mediated vasoconstriction and vasospasm in patients with atherosclerotic coronary artery disease and thus _____ _____ (have) therapeutic value.
2. Future applications of such approaches _____ _____ (consider) the most appropriate summary statistic, possibly the median intensity. (recommendation)
3. We _____ (speculation) therefore that these lanthanide metal ions _____ _____ (have) no effect on the photoluminescence and radioluminescence behavior of the structures 1 and 2.

Functional Expressions and Sentences

A. Answering the research question

* We have found that…
* We can conclude that…
* Our works indicate that…
* Our results suggest that…
* Our results indicate that…
* These results show that…
* These results have verified that…
* These results have confirmed that…
* Our studies suggest that…
* Our studies revealed that…
* Our studies have shown that…
* These observations indicate that…
* According to the results of X, we confirm that…
* X was dominated by Y, which is also evidenced by…

B. Stating unexpected outcome

* It is unexpected that…
* Interestingly, X is found to…
* However, it is surprising that…
* It might be surprising to see X.
* This is rather unexpected, since…
* A surprising observation in our study was…
* X was unexpected and not in agreement with…
* More interestingly, unexpected X was obtained.

C. Supporting the answer with results: summarizing key results

* We found that…
* In our experiments, …
* It is noteworthy that…

* *Our results confirm that...*
* *From X it is observed that...*
* *From our data, we can make a conclusion that...*

D. Supporting the answer with results: interpreting results

* *This suggests that...*
* *This indicates that...*
* *This revealed that...*
* *..., revealing that...*
* *Thus, it is clear that...*
* *X demonstrates that...*
* *..., demonstrating that...*
* *..., further confirming...*
* *By..., we verified that...*
* *It is worthy to note that...*
* *..., which may be due to...*
* *The results showed that...*
* *This provides evidence that...*
* *...can be explained as follows.*
* *This result may be ascribed to...*
* *..., which may be attributed to...*
* *X was observed, indicating that...*
* *X was observed, which confirms...*
* *By analyzing..., we concluded that...*
* *It can be seen obviously from...that...*
* *Theoretical and experimental results indicate that...*
* *According to..., X can be detected, which confirms that...*

E. Supporting the answer with results: relating results to previous research

* *This is in consistent with...*
* *..., (which is) in consistent with...*
* *This is in (good) agreement with...*
* *..., (which is) in (good) agreement with...*
* *X has also been proved by Wei and co-workers (2018).*
* *These observations agree with the results by..., assuming that...*
* *The X performance of A is also compared with previously reported Y.*

* *This value is comparable with the data reported by other groups that...*
* *X is consistent with previous literature/research/studies/reports/results.*
* *This matches well with the results in previous works, proving the importance of...*
* *X is in (good) agreement with previous literature/research/studies/reports/results.*
* *A comparison of the obtained result with available references reveals that...*

* *X expands the scope of...*
* *This is superior to X samples reported previously.*
* *The obtained results broaden the existing knowledge about...*
* *It is important to note that X does not merely surpass previous works.*

* *..., which is inconsistent with...*
* *This contradicts the hypothesis that...*
* *This contradicts previous reports which believe that...*
* *Previous works concluded that... However, our findings show that...*

F. Dealing with limitations

* *However, X is generally restricted by...*
* *Because of this potential limitation, we...*
* *However, the byproduct formation is negligible in this study.*

G. Re-summarizing results in general

* *In conclusion, ...*
* *We conclude that...*
* *In summary, we have reported that...*
* *In summary, we have demonstrated that...*
* *In summary, we synthesized and characterized a novel catalyst...*

H. Restating the answer

* *The result demonstrates that...*
* *The results above substantiate that...*
* *Therefore, it may be concluded that...*
* *In this study, X has been successfully...*
* *Overall, these results clearly indicate that...*
* *On the basis of these results, we propose that...*

Chapter 5
Discussion

I. Relating to the big issue

* *Future work here should explore...*
* *We (thus/therefore) speculate that...*
* *Thus, we expect that the probe will...*
* *In the near future, we will focus on...*
* *X will require extensive future studies...*
* *Based on these results, we envision that...*
* *In the future, X will be further optimized by...*
* *This strategy of X can be expected to be applicable to...*
* *Taking a step further, the current study further explores...*
* *Future efforts should focus on / will be dedicated toward...*
* *These results could help guide future molecular design by...*
* *Research is currently ongoing to understand the impact of...*
* *The resulting devices yielded no efficiency, suggesting that...*
* *Significantly, this work provides a feasible design strategy for...*
* *Considering its other advantages, X should be as competitive as...*
* *This discovery opens a new direction of modifications to achieve...*
* *One future development is to... Another important development is to...*
* *Finally, ... are little understood, and insights from X will be essential for...*
* *We expect in the near future an increasing attention to this field of research.*
* *X may open new opportunities for Y and thereby broaden the scope of their application.*
* *From practical applications, it remains crucial and an important research direction for...*
* *We believe that this work may contribute relevant knowledge and understanding to the future development of...*
* *The discovery of X not only proves..., but also has a great potential to...*

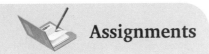

Assignments

• Reading

Read the Discussion of the article in Appendix IV. Try to find out the functional expressions and sentences according to the following model for Discussion.

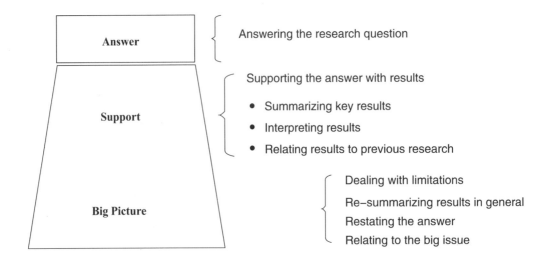

• Writing

Review what you learned in this chapter and use the above model to write a Discussion for your current or undergraduate research topic.

References

Abbate, S., Bazzini, C., Caronna, T., Fontana, F., Gangemi, F., Lebon, F, Longhi, G., Mele, A., & Natali Sora, I. (2007). Experimental and Calculated Circular Dichroism Spectra of Monoaza Helicenes. *Inorganica Chimica Acta, 360*, 908–912.

Biber, D., Johansson, S., Leech, G., Conrad, S., & Finegan, E. (1999). *Longman Grammar of Spoken and Written English.* Harlow: Pearson Education Limited.

Borja, A. (2014, June 24). 11 Steps to Structuring a Science Paper Editor Will Take Seriously. Elsevier website.

Chang, J., Wang, X., Wang, J., Li, H., & Li, F. (2019). Nucleic Acid-functionalized Metal-organic Framework-based Homogeneous Electrochemical Biosensor for Simultaneous Detection of Multiple Tumor Biomarkers. *Analytical Chemistry*, *91*, 3604–3610.

Dennis, J., White, N., Liu, R., & Buchwald, S. (2018). Palladium-catalyzed Carbon–Nitrogen (C–N) Bond Formation Has Become a Valuable Tool in the Modern Synthesis of Structurally Complex Target Molecules. *Journal of the American Chemical Society*, *140*(13), 4721–4725.

Du, Z., Zhang, X., Guo, Z., Xie, J., Dong, X., Zhu, S., Du, J., Gu, Z., & Zhao Y. (2018). X-Ray-controlled Generation of Peroxynitrite Based on Nanosized LiLuF4: Ce3+ Scintillators and Their Applications for Radiosensitization. *Advanced Materials*, *30*(43), e1804046.

Glasman-Deal, H. (2009). *Science Research Writing for Non-native Speakers of English.* London: Imperial College Press.

Herr, N., & Cunningham, J. (1999). *Hands-on Chemistry Activities with Real-life Applications.* New York: The Center for Applied Research in Education.

Liu, Y., An, S., Li, J., Kuang, Y., He, X., Guo, Y., Ma, H., Zhang, Y., Ji, Bin., & Jiang, C.

(2016). Brain-targeted Co-delivery of Therapeutic Gene and Peptide by Multifunctional Nanoparticles in Alzheimer's Disease Mice. *Biomaterials, 80*, 33–45.

Lopez, R., Wang, R., & Seelig, G. (2018). A Molecular Multi-gene Classifier for Disease Diagnostics. *Nature Chemistry, 10*, 746–754.

Lu, Z., Zhang, X., Guo, Z., Chen, Y., Mu, T., & Li, A. (2018). Total Synthesis of Aplysiasecosterol A. *Journal of the American Chemical Society, 140*(29), 9211–9218.

Pan, H. J., Huang, G., Wodrich, M. D., Tirani, F. F., Ataka, K., Shima, S., & Hu, X. (2019). A Catalytically Active [Mn]-hydrogenase Incorporating a Non-native Metal Cofactor. *Nature Chemistry, 11*(7), 669–675.

Wang, L., Yi, Y., Guo, H., & Tu, X. (2018). Atmospheric Pressure and Room Temperature Synthesis of Methanol Through Plasma-catalytic Hydrogenation of CO_2. *ACS Catalysis, 8*(1), 90–100.

Appendixes

Appendix I Keys to Exercises

Chapter 2 Introduction

Corpus in Use

I

1. Although many studies have reported the use of nitrogen doped carbon nanostructures, little research has been reported on the application of amide functionalized carbon supports.

2. Although many researchers have designed novel endcapping agents to develop new imide resins, few studies on the imide oligomers derived from fluorinated phenyethynyl-contained endcapping agents could be found in the literature.

3. Although significant progress has been made in developing RORg antagonists, the identification of novel, non-steroidal RORg antagonists for therapeutic use still remains an urgent need.

II

1. Despite the encouraging advances during the past few years, the NRR activity and selectivity are still far from satisfactory.

2. Despite researchers' considerable efforts, there has been no general and practical solution to allow for the use of amine bases in Pd-catalyzed C-N cross-coupling.

3. Despite great progress in the development and optimization of triazolylidene carbenes as catalysts for enantioselective reactions, fundamental studies of these species are relatively limited.

Writing a Research Paper in Chemistry

Lead-in Questions

1. To tell the research question or research aim and to justify the research.

2. Because an Introduction usually starts from a general picture of the research field, addresses the big issue of this field, and then is narrowed down to a specific research question or research aim.

Activity 1

A

1. b   2. d   3. a   4. c

B

1. Known: Sentences ①&②

2. Unknown: Sentence ③

3. Question: Sentence ④

4. Approach: Sentence ④

① Steroids are a large family of physiologically and pharmaceutically important natural products. ② <u>Previous studies</u> toward the chemical synthesis of steroids <u>have</u> facilitated the development of steroid based drugs. ③ <u>However</u>, the additional biological functions of structurally unusual steroids, such as Aplysiasecosterol A (1), <u>remain to be explored</u>. ④ <u>In this work, we aim to</u> explore the biology of Aplysiasecosterol A <u>by accomplishing</u> the first and asymmetric total synthesis of (1) in a convergent fashion.

C

previous studies; However; aim to; by

Activity 2

1. BI, RQ   2. RQ, BI   3. BI, RQ

Activity 3

1. Cancer diagnosis.

2. Traditional techniques cannot meet the great demand of early and accurate cancer diagnosis.

3. The reported homogeneous electrochemical techniques have several drawbacks.

4. It was divided into three aspects by using sequential expressions *First*, *Second*, and *Third*.

5. To develop a label-free and enzyme-free homogeneous electrochemical strategy for ultrasensitive and simultaneous detection of multiple tumor biomarkers.

6. The research aim is to develop a cancer diagnosis technique with three traits: label-free, enzyme-free, and able to do multiple tumor biomarker detection. These traits are respectively aimed at the three aspects of drawbacks mentioned in the knowledge gap.

Activity 4

A

To establish the significance of the research topic, introduce key terms, and identify the big issue.

B

Significance: Sentences ①&②

Key term: steroids

Big issue: Sentence ③

Activity 5

A

Research interest: extensively studied, be studied for centuries, enormous interest

Usefulness: a promising tool, a powerful technology, useful method

Economic reasons: economically important, low-cost, economically friendly

Importance: vital for, of great importance, key role

B

1. extensively studied   2. key role   3. a promising tool

4. of great importance 5. economically friendly 6. enormous interest

Activity 6

A

Text A: however, ...has significant shortcomings, including…

Text B: Despite…, …remain to be explored.

B

1. However, a major problem 2. Despite, there is much room

3. Although, several limitations 4. However, remains unconquered

5. not, yet, rarely 6. However, remains challenging

Activity 7

A

b　a　d　c

B

1. Overview of Previous Studies 2. Specific Studies 3. Knowledge Gap

4. Framing the Knowledge Gap 5. Funnel

Activity 8

A

<u>Despite</u> these notable advances, methods for highly enantioselective N-alkylation (nonallylic alkylation) of indoles with broad substrate scope <u>remain rare</u>.

B

However, few studies/investigations/attempts/researchers…

However, little research/work/information/attention...

Appendixes

C

1. However, little research has been reported on the application of amide functionalized carbon supports.

2. However, few studies/investigations/attempts are carried out directly using cor-rosive biofilm in the rust layer.

3. However, little research/attention has been focused on the utilization of sulfone units in helicene synthesis.

4. To our knowledge, however, few studies/investigations/attempts have been carried out on the correlation between the microstructure and gas separation performance of polyimide membranes.

5. However, there are relatively few studies/investigations/attempts about the influence of anions on the crystal structures of L so far.

Activity 9

Research aim: Herein, we aim to achieve…

Research question: In this work, we wish to examine whether and to what extent…

Hypothesis: We hypothesized that…

Experimental approach: through the less invasive intravenous administration by…

Activity 10

A (possible answers)

1. In this work, we examine whether PhABCG1 is involved in VOC emission.

2. The purpose of this study is to determine the preferred pathways for CH_3OH formation from CO_2.

3. Herein, we investigate what types of Pd-Cu bimetallic alloy structures on the surface facilitate CO_2 hydrogenation to CH_3OH.

4. In this study we hypothesized that both transmittance and reflectance spectra are appropriate for sensing experiments with these MCM structures.

B

1. identify   2. test   3. design   4. explore/analyze   5. report   6. analyze/explore

Activity 11

A

1. c   2. d   3. b   4. a

B (possible answers)

1. The purpose of this study is to determine the samples' effect on the resistance to carbon deposition and catalytic activity. For this purpose, we tested these samples prepared with glycine, urea and without fuel.

2. In this study we hypothesized that it should be possible to impregnate a synthetically fluorinated NO donor into fluoropolymers. To test this hypothesis, we used the simple solvent-swelling method.

C

1. The purpose of this study is to determine the samples' effect on the resistance to carbon deposition and catalytic activity by testing these samples prepared with glycine, urea and without fuel.

2. In this study we hypothesized that it should be possible to impregnate a synthetically fluorinated NO donor into fluoropolymers using the simple solvent-swelling method.

Chapter 3   Methods

Corpus in Use

1. in, in   2. at   3. in   4. in   5. in   6. from/through   7. with/to   8. at

9. at   10. from   11. with   12. by, by, with

Lead-in Questions

1. Because Methods is about things they have already done.

2. To tell the reader how the research question is answered.

Activity 1

A

5. e   3. a   1. f   4. b   8. d   6. c   9. h   2. g   7. i

B

Past simple and passive voice are mainly used. Past simple is used to describe things that were already done. When reading a Methods section, readers care more about what was done instead of who did it, so passive voice is used to make the text less personal. This also implies that any researcher can repeat the research by using the same methods.

Present simple is also used. This is either to show a fact (*The sites were selected from the London Basin area, which* is *located in…*) or to describe a standard procedure or methods (*This method* obtains *a precipitate through…*).

Activity 2

1. The electrical signals were recorded.

2. The frequency of the power supply was fixed.

3. Plasma hydrogenation of CO_2 were carried out.

4. The change of the gas volume before and after the reaction was measured.

5. To evaluate the reaction performance of CO_2 hydrogenation to methanol, the concentration of major products in the condensate was calculated.

Activity 3

1. Plasma hydrogenation of CO_2 was carried out using different DBD reactors at atmospheric pressure.

2. A mixture of H_2 and CO_2 was fed into the DBD reactor at a total flow rate of 40 ml/min.

3. In this work, the discharge power was calculated by using the Q-U Lissajous method and was fixed at 10 W.

4. The gaseous products were analyzed using a gas chromatograph equipped with a thermal

conductivity detector (TCD) and a flame ionized detector (FID).

Activity 4

1. Prior to   2. subsequently   3. After   4. next   5. When   6. first step

7. At the end of

Activity 5

1. three times   2. slowly   3. carefully   4. quickly   5. tightly, to prevent

6. under identical conditions, every

Chapter 4　Results

Corpus in Use

I

Students' own answers.

II

Verbs in Results section	Noun (noun structure)	*that*-clause
observe	Y	Y
show	Y	Y
use	Y	N
obtain	Y	N
find	Y	Y
report	Y	Y
calculate	Y	N
compare	Y	N
prepare	Y	N
determine	Y	Y

Appendixes

Lead-in Questions

One picture is worth a thousand words. This is why visual illustrations are useful and important when writing the Results section.

Activity 1

Types	Uses	Example
diagram	d	E
table	f	B
map	a	F
pie chart	c	D
bar graph	b	C
line graph	e	A

Activity 2

A

The table contains statistic data, while the figure only contains visual illustration. The table legend is above the table, while the figure legend is on the bottom.

B

It depends on your objectives. If you want to stress numbers, you can present your data as table. If you want to compare gradients, you can show your data as figure. But never duplicate the information you already described by using both table and figure.

Activity 3

A

Data: c, example 1; Results: a, example 3; Implication: b, example 2

B

Data

Results that don't fit hypothesis

Research aim

Statistical analysis

Experimental results

C

It depends on whether the presentation of data helps answer the research question.

Activity 4

A

1. c   2. a   3. b   4. d

B

2   3   1

Activity 5

1. The size distribution of GNP has an average size of 60 \xA1\xC0 9 nm together with a typical TEM image as an inset (Figure 1).

2. The crystal habit is clearly reflected on the crystal structure of the solids (Figure 2).

3. Clearly, the alloy formation could considerably decrease the crystallite size of the Cu phase (Table 3).

Activity 6

A

1. Adding H_2O_2 to convert GSH into GSSG significantly enhances fluorescence (Figure 1).

2. The electrochemical testing does not change the chemical states of CoP/NCNHP catalyst.

B

1. After adding H_2O_2 to convert GSH into GSSG, a significant fluorescence enhancement was observed (Figure 1).

2. According to an electrochemical testing, chemical states of CoP/NCNHP catalyst are nearly not changed.

Appendixes

C

1. When H_2O_2 was added to convert GSH into GSSG, a significant fluorescence enhancement was observed (Figure 1).

2. When we completed a desired catalytic reaction, magnetic stir bars could then be easily separated from the reaction mixture.

Chapter 5 Discussion

Corpus in Use

Students' own answers.

Lead-in Questions

1. The information in the Results section highlights the key research findings. The Discussion section explains what the results mean and how they move research in the area forward. The Discussion section also relates the current research to previous research.

2. A Discussion focuses on interpreting the results. A Conclusion is a short summary of the whole research article.

Activity 1

1. Answering the research question

2. Supporting the answer with results

3. Interpreting the results

4. Re-summarizing the results in general

5. Relating to the big picture

Activity 2

A (possible answers)

1. This study shows that PhABCG1 is involved in VOC emission.

2. Our results indicate that Mn addition does not promote the formation of olefins.

3. In this study, we have shown that both transmittance and reflectance spectra are appropriate for sensing experiments with these MCM structures.

B (possible answer)

This study shows that exposing oilseed rape seeds to neonicotinoids affects reproductive potential in wild bee populations.

Activity 3

A

The result presented in Discussion is a summary (Neonicotinoid treatment decreased the number of queens in wild bee populations.) and interpretation (Sublethal amount of neonicotinoids may have harmful effects on the reproduction of wild bees.) of the result in Results.

B

This study shows that exposing oilseed rape seeds to neonicotinoids affects reproductive potential in wild bee populations. <u>We found that / In our experiments,</u> neonicotinoid treatment decreased the number of queens in wild bee populations. Sublethal amount of neonicotinoids may have harmful effects on the reproduction of wild bees.

C (possible answer)

This decrease implies that sublethal amount of neonicotinoids may have harmful effects on the reproduction of wild bees.

D (possible answer)

We found that there was a significant correlation between the bacterial community composition and soil pH. This finding indicates that pH is an important predictor of the community composition.

Activity 4

A

1. expand (broaden)   2. confirm (is consistent with)   3. contradict (is in stark contrast to)

Appendixes

B

1. comparable to   2. contradict   3. good agreement with   4. expand

C (possible answer)

We found that there was a significant correlation between the bacterial community composition and soil pH. This suggests that pH is an important predictor of the community composition, which is consistent with Porter et al.'s study (2017). However, our finding contrasts with earlier findings that pH showed no significant correlation with bacterial community composition (Snow et al., 2012).

Activity 5

Summarizing results: ① ②

Restating the answer: ③

Relating to the big issue: ④

Activity 6

A

1. b   2. d   3. c   4. a

B

1. implication (imply)   2. recommendation (should)

3. application (be applicable to)   4. speculation (speculate)

C

1. imply/suggest; may/might antagonize; may/might have

2. should consider

3. speculate; may/might have

Appendix II Common Affixes in Chemistry

Affix	Meaning	Example
a-	not, without	amorphous 无定形的 asymmetric 非对称的
alkal-	soda ash, alkali	alkaline 碱性的；含碱的 alkali metal 碱金属
allo-	other, different	allogene 异基因 allotrope 同素异形体
amin-	ammonia	amine 胺基 amino acid 氨基酸
amph-	double, on both sides	amphibian 两栖动物；两栖的 amphoteric 两性的（酸性的或碱性的）
anti-	against, opposite	antibiotics 抗生素 antiseptic 防腐的
aqu-	water	aquatic 水生的 aqueous solution 水溶液
baro-	pressure	barometer 气压表 barometric 气压的
bi-	two	bichloride 二氯化物 binary compound 二元化合物
bio-	life	biochemistry 生物化学 biosynthesis 生物合成
carbo-	coal, carbon	carbohydrate 碳水化合物 carbonate 碳酸盐
chem-	chemistry	chemical 化学品 chemotherapy 化学疗法
com-	with, together	composition 组成 compound 化合物
conjug-	joined together	conjugate acid 共轭酸 conjugation reaction 结合反应
cosm-	the world or universe	cosmic ray 宇宙射线 cosmochemistry 宇宙化学；天体化学
cry-	cold	cryesthesia 冷觉过敏 cryogenic 冷冻的；低温的
de-	down, without, from	decomposition 分解；腐烂 dehydrate 脱水；去水

(Continued)

Affix	Meaning	Example
dens-	thick	density 密度 densimeter 密度计
di-	separate, double, across	dioxide 二氧化物 disaccharide 二糖
dis-	separate, apart	disappear 消失 dissociation 离解（作用）
duct-	lead	ductal 管的；导管的 ductile 易延展的
electr-	electrode	electron 电子 electrolyte 电解质；电解液
elem-	basic	element 元素 elementary 初级的；简单的
en-	in, into	endothermic 吸热的
equ-	equal	equation 等式；方程式 equilibrium 化学平衡
exo-	out, outside, without	exothermic 放热的
ferr-	iron	ferrite 铁氧体 ferromagnetism 磁铁性
fiss-	cleft, split	fission 裂变；分裂
flu-	flow	fluctuate 波动 fluids 流体
fract-	break, broken	fracture 断裂；断口 fractional distillation 分馏
gen-	bear, produce, beginning	gene 基因 genome 基因组；染色体组
glyc-	sweet	glycogen 糖原；动物淀粉 glycolysis 糖酵解 glycolipid 糖脂类
graph-	write, writing	graphite 石墨 graphene 石墨烯
halo-	salt	halogen 卤素 halometer 盐量计
hetero-	other, different	heterogeneity 异质性；非均匀性 heterogeneous mixture 不均匀混合物 heterovalent 多价的

(Continued)

Affix	Meaning	Example
hom-	same, alike	homogeneity 同质性；均匀性 homogeneous mixture 均匀混合物 homokaryon 同核体
hybrid-	mongrel, hybrid, combination	hybrid orbital 杂化轨道 hybridization 杂交
hydr-	water	hydration 水合作用 hydrolysis 水解作用
hyper-	over, above, excessive	hyperplastic 增生的 hyperspectral image 高光谱图像
hypo-	under, beneath	hypochlorous acid 次氯酸 hypoderm 皮下组织；下皮
im-	not	immiscible 不相溶的 impermeable 不渗透的
in-	in, into	inactive 不活泼的 inorganic 无机的
iso-	equal	isohydric 等氢离子的 isomer 同分异构体
kine-	move, moving, movement	kinematics 运动学 kinetics 动力学 kinetic energy 动能
lip-	fat	lipase 脂肪酶 lipoprotein 脂蛋白
liqu-	fluid, liquid	liquefy 液化 liquable 可液化的
macro-	large, long	macromolecule 大分子
malle-	hammer	malleable 有延展性的 malleableize 韧化
meta-	between, change	metabolism 代谢
misc-	mix	miscible 可溶混的 miscibility 溶混性
mono-	single, one	monomer 单体 monoxide 一氧化物 carbon monoxide 一氧化碳
morph-	form	morphology 形态学 morphactin 形态素；整形素

(Continued)

Affix	Meaning	Example
neo-	new, recent	neonate 新生儿 neoantigen 新抗原
non-	not	nonpolar 非极性的
nuc-	nut, center	nuciform 坚果状的；核子状的 nucleus 原子核；细胞核
oct-	eight	octane 辛烷 octet rule 八隅规则
orbi-	circle	orbicular 球状的 orbital 轨道的
oxid-	oxygen	oxide 氧化物 oxidizer 氧化剂
photo-	light	photochemical smog 光化雾 photon 光子 photosynthesis 光合作用
polar-	of the pole, polarity	polar covalent 极性共价 polarity 极性
poly-	many	polymer 聚合物 polysulfide 多硫化物
pro-	forward, positive, for, in front of	prochiral 前手性的 proton 质子
quant-	how much	quantitative 量化的；定量的 quantum 量子；量子的
radi-	ray, radius	radiation 辐射 radioactive 放射性的
sali-	salt	saline 盐的；生理盐水 salinity 盐度；盐分
solu-	dissolve	solubility 溶解度；可溶性 solution 溶液
spect-	see, look at	spectrum 光谱；波谱 spectator ions 旁观离子
syn-	together, with	synthesize 合成；结合 synthetic 合成的；人造的
therm-	heat	thermal 热的；热量的 thermochemistry 热化学 thermometer 温度计

(Continued)

Affix	Meaning	Example
trans-	across, through	transisomer 反式异构体 transition elements 过渡元素
un-	not	uncatalyzed 非催化的 undamped 无阻尼的 unsaturated 不饱和的
vapor-	steam, vapor	vaporability 挥发性；汽化性 vaporization 蒸发
vulcan-	fire	vulcanize 硫化 vulcanizer 硫化剂
-ane	single covalent bond	methane 甲烷 ethane 乙烷 propane 丙烷
-ene	double covalent bond	ethylene 乙烯 polypropylene 聚丙烯
-ide	a chemical made up of two or more elements	sodium chloride 氯化钠 hydroxide 氢氧化物
-ion	process	fusion 聚变；融合 diffusion 扩散
-lysis	loose, loosening, breaking	analysis 分析 electrolysis 电解
-oid	like, form	alkaloid 生物碱 metalloid 类金属的
-mer	part	dimer 二聚物 trimer 三聚物
-meter	measure	calorimeter 热量计 fluidimeter 粘度计；流度计
-thesis	an arranging, statement	hypothesis 假设 synthesis 合成
-yne	triple covalent bond	benzyne 苯炔 ethyne 乙炔

Source: Adapted from Herr, N., & Cunningham, J. (1999). *Hands-on Chemistry Activities with Real-life Applications*. New York: The Center for Applied Research in Education.

Appendix III Common Chemical Abbreviations and Acronyms

Å	angstrom
A	absorbance
α	observed rotation
[α]	specific rotation (units (deg•mL)/(g•dm) are understood)
abs	absolute
Ac	acetyl
acac	acetylacetonate
AcOH	acetic acid
Ac2O	acetic anhydride
AIBN	azobisisobutyronitrile
Ala	alanine
AM1	Austin model 1 (semiempirical MM method)
AMP	adenosine 5'-monophosphate
amu	atomic mass units
Anal.	combustion elemental analysis
anhyd	anhydrous
aq	aqueous
Ar	aryl
atm	atmosphere
ATP	adenosine-5'-triphosphate
ATR	attenuated total reflectance
au	atomic units
av	average

9-BBN-H	9-borabicyclo[3.3.1]nonane
BET	Brunauer-Emmett-Teller (absorption isotherm)
BINAP	2,2'-bis(diphenylphosphanyl)-1,1'-binaphthyl
bipy	2,2'-bipyridine or 2,2'-bipyridyl

(Continued)

Bn	benzyl (PhCH2 also Bzl)
Boc	tert-butoxycarbonyl
bp	boiling point
bpy	2,2'-bipyridine or 2,2'-bipyridyl
Br	bromine
br	broad (spectral peak)
BSA	bovine serum albumin
Bu	butyl
BuLi	butyl lithium (also n-BuLi)
Bz	benzoyl (PhCO also bz)

°C	degrees Celsius
calcd	calculated (for MS analysis)
cAMP	adenosine cyclic 3',5'-phosphate
CAN	ceric ammonium nitrate
cat	catalytic
CBZ, Cbz	benzyloxycarbonyl (protecting group)
CC	coupled cluster (computational method)
cc	cubic centimeters
CD	circular dichroism
cDNA	circular DNA
c-Hex	cyclohexyl (Thieme Cy)
CI	chemical ionization
CIF	crystallographic information file
Cl	chlorine
cm	centimeter
cm^{-1}	wavenumbers(s)
cmc	critical micelle concentration
13C NMR	carbon NMR
cod	1,5-cyclooctadiene

(Continued)

compd	compound
concn	concentration
COSY	correlation spectroscopy (2D NMR method)
Cp	cyclopentadienyl
Cp	heat capacity at constant pressure
CPK	Corey-Pauling-Koltun (models)
CP/MAS	cross-polarization/magic angle spinning (NMR)
cryst	crystalline
CSA	camphorsulfonic acid
CT	charge transfer
CV	cyclic voltammetry

δ	chemical shift (ppm) downfield from TMS
d	days; doublet (spectral)
d	density
D	debye
D	diffusion coefficient
DABCO	1,4-diazabicyclo[2.2.2]octane
dansyl	5-(dimethylamino)-1-naphthalenesulfonyl
DBN	1,5-diazabicyclo[4.3.0]non-5-ene
DBU	1,8-diazabicyclo[5.4.0]undec-7-ene
DCC	N,N'-dicyclohexylcarbodiimide
DCE	1,2-dichloroethane
DCM	use CH2Cl2 instead
DDQ	2,3-dichloro-5,6-dicyano-1,4-benzoquinone
de	diastereomeric excess
DEAD	diethyl azodicarboxylate
dec	decomposition (for mp)
DIAD	diisopropyl azodicarboxylate
DIBALH	diisobutylaluminum hydride

(Continued)

DIC	diisopropylcarbodiimide
dil	dilute
DIPEA	N,N-diisopropylethylamine
DMA	dimethylacetamide
DMAP	4-(N,N-dimethylamino)pyridine
DME	1,2-dimethoxyethane
DMF	dimethylformamide
DMP	Des-Martin periodinane
DMPU	N,N'-dimethylpropylene urea
DMSO	dimethylsulfoxide
DMTrCl	4,4-dimethoxytrityl chloride
dp	degree of polymerization
DPPA	diphenylphosphoryl azide
DPS	tert-butyldiphenylsilyl
dr	diastereomeric ratio
DTT	dithiothreitol

ε	molar absorptivity
ee	enantiomeric excess
EDC or EDCI	N-ethyl-N'-(3-dimethylaminopropyl)carbodiimide
EDTA	ethylenediaminetetraacetic acid
EGDMA	ethylene glycol dimethacrylate
EI	electron impact
EPR	electron paramagnetic resonance
eq	equation
equiv	equivalents
ESI	electrospray ionization
Et	ethyl
Et3N	triethylamine (use instead of TEA)
eu	entropy units

(Continued)

FAB	fast atom bombardment (in MS)
Fc	ferrocenyl
Fmoc	9-fluorenylmethoxycarbonyl
fp	freezing point
FT	Fourier transform
g	gram(s); gas
G	gauss
G	Gibbs free energy
GC	gas chromatography
h	hours(s)
h	Planck constant
H	henry (units)
H	enthalpy
HMDS	hexamethyldisilazane
HMPA	hexamethylphosphoric triamide
H NMR	proton NMR
HOMO	highest occupied molecular orbital
HPLC	high-performance liquid chromatography
HRMS	high-resolution mass spectrometry
HNMR	proton NMR
insol	insoluble
IR	infrared
isc	intersystem crossing
J	Joule
J	coupling constant in NMR

(Continued)

k	kilo
k	rate constant; Boltzmann constant
K	Kelvin
K	equilibrium constant
KHMDS	potassium hexamethyldisilazide
l	liquid
L	liter; ligand
LAH	lithium aluminum hydride
LDA	lithium diisopropylamide
LHMDS	lithium hexamethyldisilazane
lit.	literature value
λ_{max}	max UV-vis wavelength
LUMO	lowest unoccupied molecular orbital
m	meter; milli; multiplet (spectral)
M	molar (moles per liter)
M+	parent molecular ion (in MS)
μ	micro
max	maximum
m-CPBA	meta-chloroperoxybenzoic acid
MAA	methacrylic acid
MALDI	matrix-assisted laser desorption ionization (in MS)
Me	methyl
MeCN	acetonitrile
MEK	methyl ethyl ketone
MEMCl	2-methoxyethoxymethyl chloride
Mes	mesityl (2,4,6-trimethylphenyl)
MHz	megahertz
min	minute(s); minimum

(Continued)

MIP	molecularly imprinted polymer
mL	milliliter
mm	millimeter
mM	millimolar (moles per liter)
mmol	millimole(s)
MMA	methyl methacrylate
MN	number average molecular weight
mo	month
mol	mole(s)
mol wt	molecular weight
MOM	methoxymethyl
mp	melting point
MS	mass spectrometry; molecular sieves
Ms	mesyl (methanesulfonyl)
MTBE	methyl tert-butyl ether
MVK	methyl vinyl ketone
MW	weight average molecular weight
m/z	mass to charge ratio (in MS)

N	normal (equiv per liter)
NADH	nicotinamide adenine dinucleotide hydride
n-Bu	normal butyl (primary)
NBS	N-bromosuccinimide
NCS	N-chlorosuccinimide
NMO	N-methylmorpholine N-oxide
NMP	N-methyl-2-pyrrolidinone
NMR	nuclear magnetic resonance
NOE	nuclear overhauser effect
no.	number
Nu	nucleophile

(Continued)

obsd	observed
OD	optical density
op	optical purity
oxdn	oxidation

Pa	Pascal
PBS	phosphate-buffered saline
PCC	pyridinium chlorochromate
PDC	pyridinium dichromate
PEG	polyethylene glycol
PET	photoinduced electron transfer
pH	proton log units
Ph	phenyl
Phth	phthaloyl
PMB	p-methoxybenzyl
PPA	polyphosphoric acid
pp	pages
ppm	part per million
ppt	precipitate
Pr	propyl
PTSA	p-toluenesulfonic acid
Pv	pivaloyl
py	pyridine

q	quartet (spectral)
quin	quintet (spectral)

R	gas constant
R	alkyl group

(Continued)

RCM	ring-closing metathesis
recryst	recrystallized
red	reduction
Red-Al®	sodium bis (2-methoxyethoxy) aluminum hydride
redox	reduction-oxidation
rel	relative
Rf	retention factor (in chromatography)
ROMP	ring-opening metathesis polymerization
rt	room temperature (Thieme publishing r.t.)

s	seconds; singlet (spectral); solid
S	entropy
SAR	structure-activity relationship
sat.	saturated
s-Bu	sec-butyl
SD	standard deviation
SE	standard error
SEM	scanning electron microscope
sept	septet (spectral)
SET	single electron transfer
sext	sextet (spectral)
sh	sharp (spectral), shoulder (spectral)
SN1	unimolecular nucleophilic substitution
sol	solid
soln	solution

t	triplet (spectral)
t	time or temp in °C
T	temperature in kelvin
t-Bu	tert-butyl

(Continued)

TBS	tert-butyldimethylsilyl
temp	temperature
TES	triethylsilane
TCE	2,2,2-trichloroethyl
TCNE	tetracyanoethylene
Tf	trifluoromethanesulfonyl (triflyl)
TFA	trifluoroacetic acid
TFAA	trifluoroacetic anhydride
THF	tetrahydrofuran
THP	tetrahydropyran
TIPS	triisopropylsilyl
TLC	thin-layer chromatography
TMEDA	N,N,N',N'-tetramethyl-1,2-ethylenediamine
TMS	trimethylsilyl or tetramethylsilane
TOF	time of flight (in MS)
Tol	toluene
tosyl	p-toluenesulfonyl
TPS	triphenylsilyl
t_R	retention time (in chromatography)
Tr	triphenylmethyl (trityl)
Troc	2,2,2-trichloroethyl chloroformate
trityl	triphenylmethyl
Ts	p-toluenesulfonyl (tosyl)
TS	transition state

UV-vis	ultraviolet-visible absorption spectroscopy

VDW	van der Waals (interaction)
vis	visible
vol	volume

(Continued)

vs.	versus
v/v	volume to volume ratio |//
wt	weight
w/w	weight to weight ratio
X-ray	X-ray (capital X)

Appendix IV   Model Research Article

A Molecular Multi-gene Classifier for Disease Diagnostics[1,2]

Randolph Lopez, Ruofan Wang and Georg Seelig

Introduction[3]

Gene expression changes are associated with every human disease. Monitoring such changes enables clinicians to perform diagnosis, evaluate therapeutic efficacy and predict disease recurrence. Existing methods for high-throughput RNA detection such as quantitative reverse transcription PCR (RT-qPCR), microarrays or RNA sequencing can in principle be used to quantitatively monitor gene expression changes in diagnostic applications, but they remain cost-prohibitive in situations where recurrent monitoring or regular screenings are necessary. Moreover, the experimental complexity and the need for in silico computational analysis of the resulting data mean that such tests can only be performed in specialized laboratory settings. To overcome these limitations of complexity and cost it is necessary to develop instrument-free diagnostic tests that can be administered and interpreted directly at the point of care.

In the past two decades, researchers have found that peripheral gene expression (for example, whole blood, platelets, exosomes, plasma or saliva) is consistently altered between cancer patients and healthy controls. For instance, relative quantitation of telomerase reverse transcriptase (hTERT) RNA in blood or serum has diagnostic and prognostic value in many different cancer types. Researchers have also demonstrated that a classifier based on a patient's blood RNA profile can distinguish between bacterial and viral infections. Discriminating between these two groups is essential to address inappropriate prescription of antibiotics and combat antibiotic resistance. Importantly, early cancer diagnostics and combating antimicrobial resistance are just two examples of medical applications that would benefit from rapid and inexpensive gene expression diagnostics for use at home or the point of care.

---

1 The main purpose of including this model is to help students understand the logic of research papers and identify functional expressions and sentences, so the figures in this article have been omitted.

2 Journals have different format guidelines, so it is common to see variations of the IMRD structure. For example, *Nature Chemistry*, from which this article was chosen, specifically requires Methods to be the last section rather than the second section of the main text. You may also see this organization in other journals.

3 *Nature Chemistry* also requires an Introduction without heading. This heading was added by the author of this book.

Recent work in cell-free synthetic biology and DNA nano-technology has demonstrated progress towards the goal of creating low-cost RNA diagnostics. For example, a test for Zika virus has been developed by embedding a set of engineered molecular components for RNA sensing and signal amplification in a paper matrix. Detection of the RNA marker is converted into a colorimetric signal that allows intuitive interpretation. However, to broaden the utility of such tests beyond applications where detection of a single marker is sufficient, it will be necessary to develop "molecular computation" technologies that can convert information encoded in multi-gene expression signatures into interpretable yes/no answers.

Cell-free molecular circuits with dozens of interconnected components have been experimentally demonstrated and provide proof of principle that complex computation can be embedded in molecular substrates. However, rationally designed molecular circuits realized so far are not well matched to diagnostic applications. For instance, it is often assumed that inputs take Boolean values (high or low), an assumption that is not naturally compatible with RNA inputs derived from a biological sample. In contrast, computational gene expression classifiers are commonly built using logistic regression, support vector machines (SVMs) or neural network approaches that take better advantage of the information encoded in the actual levels of the biomolecules of interest. Finally, inputs are typically short, unstructured oligonucleotides with carefully designed sequences rather than long biological RNAs with extensive secondary structure. To realize the potential of DNA computation for diagnostic applications it is thus necessary to develop molecular classifiers that operate directly on RNA inputs and produce a result rapidly and robustly.

Here, we address this challenge and demonstrate a framework for creating a DNA-based molecular "computer" capable of performing multi-gene classification (Fig. 1a). In our workflow, publicly available, labelled (for example, bacterial infection vs viral infection) gene expression data are first used to train an in silico linear classifier, specifically an SVM. During training, constraints are imposed to find the minimal set of genes that need to be considered for classification with a desired accuracy. The resulting model consists of a set of input features (the RNA transcripts), a positive or negative weight associated with each feature, and a set of mathematical operations (summation and comparison to a threshold) performed over these inputs. Once an optimal model has been obtained, a computational tool translates all parameters and mathematical functions into a novel class of DNA probes that realize the classifier at the molecular level. In the following, we first test each molecular classifier component individually, starting with RNA detection and assignment of weights. Finally, we validate the entire workflow by implementing molecular classifiers for the two applications introduced above, namely early cancer diagnostics based on ratiometric detection of hTERT, and distinguishing between bacterial and viral infections based on a panel of host genes.

Results

Detection of transcripts through assisted hybridization. The first step in our implementation of a molecular classifier is the detection of RNA transcripts (Fig. 1b). Initially, we pursued an approach using competitive hybridization (or strand displacement) probes at room temperature (Supplementary Section 2 and Supplementary Fig. 1). However, we found that the high degree of secondary structure in RNA transcripts severely limited the probe binding efficiency. The use of computational tools for identifying unstructured stretches of RNA ameliorated the situation somewhat, but binding kinetics still varied widely (Supplementary Fig. 2). Moreover, the number of potential probe binding sites on a transcript was determined entirely by the secondary structure and could not be tuned at will, which is incompatible with our molecular computation scheme, as described in the section "Molecular implementation of weights".

To enable robust detection of a larger number of target regions within a transcript, we developed an assisted hybridization protocol. Specifically, we designed a two-stage reaction whereby an input sequence within the target RNA transcript (domain a) is thermally or chemically annealed to a hybridization probe consisting of two partially complementary strands (Fig. 1c). Additional helper strands (60 nt) are included in the reaction. Helper strands hybridize adjacent to the targeted region on the RNA to further help unfold its secondary structure and to prevent binding between the adjacent RNA regions and the single-stranded domain of the hybridization probe. As a result of this initial reaction the longer probe strand becomes attached to the transcript and a short toehold (domain t1*) is exposed within that strand. Domain a* in the hybridization probe is partially double-stranded (15 nt single-stranded and 15 nt double-stranded) and is complementary to the target sequence. On binding to its target, hybridization results in a maximum overall gain of 9 bp, making this reaction thermodynamically favourable. Subsequently, a fluorescent reporter is added to the solution and reacts with the bound strand through toehold-mediated strand displacement, resulting in an increase in fluorescence. If the target RNA is not present, the translator probe reforms upon annealing and cannot interact with the fluorescent reporter. Importantly, because of the two-stage design, the target sequence on the transcript is completely independent of the reporter sequence.

To experimentally test this strategy, we designed hybridization probes to target three different regions of an mRNA coding for the fusion protein histone 2B Citrine (Citrine) as well as a control hybridization probe specific to GAPDH. For an initial test of the probe design with an unstructured target, a short oligonucleotide encoding the target sequence (30 nM) was added to each probe at room temperature. As designed, addition of the target oligonucleotide resulted in increased signal from a downstream fluorescent reporter (Fig. 1d). In contrast, addition of in vitro transcribed Citrine RNA (30 nM) did not result in increased fluorescence, because the secondary structure of the RNA transcript hindered the strand displacement reaction. We then tested whether addition of the helper strands could aid hybridization between the RNA target and probe at room temperature, but we observed significant triggering for only one hybridization probe (Supplementary Fig. 3).

Subsequently, we implemented a thermal annealing strategy where the hybridization probe and corresponding helper strands were annealed with the Citrine RNA transcript before addition of the fluorescent reporter. Thermal annealing was performed by heating reactants to 70 °C for 10 s and subsequently cooling to 25 °C at a rate of −1 °C per 10s. As expected, we observed a fluorescent response equivalent to the concentration of added transcript in all Citrine probes while the GAPDH probe showed no increased in fluorescence (Fig. 1e). We carried out the same reaction without addition of helper strands and we observed a lower fluorescence response across all conditions. These results suggest that the helper strands have a role in suppressing non-specific binding between single-stranded overhangs in the probe and single-stranded domains in the RNA target. We also observed very little increase in fluorescence in the case where no transcript was added. Moreover, we performed thermal annealing experiments in a background of cellular mRNA extracted from HEK293 cells without observing any unspecific triggering (Supplementary Fig. 4).

Thermal annealing is not ideal for point-of-care diagnostic applications, so we also implemented a chemical denaturing strategy for unfolding RNA targets. Following previous work, we evaluated the use of urea and subsequent addition of $MgCl_2$ as a method to denature and renature nucleic acid base pairing. We implemented this chemical annealing strategy by incubating a hybridization probe, helper strands and the corresponding target in 6.4 M urea for 15 min followed by incubation with Mg^{2+} for 15 min. We observed a target-specific increase in fluorescence equivalent to thermal annealing conditions when adding the Citrine RNA transcript or a target oligonucleotide (Fig. 1f).

We note that this assisted hybridization strategy is quite distinct from earlier work in dynamic DNA nanotechnology that generally aimed to create fully autonomous systems that require minimal intervention from an experimentalist. However, we found that separating the detection reaction into an annealing step followed by a more conventional strand displacement-based reporter reaction improved not only the robustness of input detection but also dramatically accelerated it. Both features are crucial for designing a practical diagnostic test.

Molecular implementation of weights. In a gene expression classifier, RNA transcripts have varying levels of influence on the classifier outcome. In silico, every transcript is assigned a numerical weight capturing its importance (Fig. 2a). At the molecular level, we implemented these weights by designing multiple hybridization probes that target different regions within each RNA. For example, weights n = 1, 2, N are realized by having 1, 2 or N distinct probes targeting the same transcript (Fig. 2b). Even though the targeted sequences on the transcript are different, each probe contains an identical output strand (domains t1*x* in Fig. 1c), which then triggers a fluorescent reporter. Every additional hybridization probe results in a proportional increase in the steady-state fluorescence signal. The fluorescence due to mRNA1 should thus be proportional to the product w1*[mRNA1], where w1 is an integer weight and [mRNA1] is the concentration of mRNA1.

We implemented this set-up experimentally by designing reactions with 1, 2, 3 or 4 probes targeting contiguous regions on the Citrine transcript. To avoid saturation of the reporter complex, we operated the system in a regime where reporter and hybridization probes far exceeded the transcript concentration. We measured the fluorescence signal corresponding to the reporter complex before and after addition of the hybridized probe–RNA complexes until a steady state was reached (Fig. 2c). As expected, we found that the steady-state signal was linearly proportional to the number of hybridization probes bound to the RNA transcript for all RNA concentrations tested, demonstrating that this mechanism can be used to assign an integer-valued weight to an RNA transcript (Fig. 2d).

Summation and thresholding. Building a complete linear classifier requires a mechanism for summing up weights and comparing the sum to a threshold value to obtain the desired yes/no answer (Fig. 3a). If there are multiple transcripts with different weights of the same sign, we can compute the sum of their contributions simply by using the same output sequence across all probes. The total concentration of output strands and thus the final fluorescence signal is then proportional to the sum w1*[mRNA1] + ... + wN*[mRNAN].

Weights with negative values can be implemented using a distinct output sequence for the negative probes. The sums of negative and positive weights in a classifier are then represented by the total concentrations of two distinct output strands.

To complete the summation, the individual sums of positive and negative weights—represented by (positive) concentrations of two distinct nucleic acids sequences—need to be subtracted from one another. Intuitively, such a subtraction can be realized as a chemical reaction whereby stoichiometric amounts of positive and negative output strands annihilate each other until only the majority species is left. The concentration of that species then is the final result of the summation over all weights. To implement such a stoichiometric annihilation reaction between two nucleic acid species of unrelated sequence, we take advantage of the cooperative hybridization mechanism ("annihilator" gate) introduced by Zhang.

The final step in the molecular computation pipeline is to compare the result of the summation to a threshold value. In the simplest case, the threshold value is set to zero and the class a specific input sample belongs to is determined simply by the sign of the final sum. Non-zero threshold values can be realized by spiking the corresponding amount of negative or positive output strand into the reaction, which biases the sum by a controlled amount.

Molecular thresholding of RNA transcripts. To experimentally test whether an off-the-shelf thresholding (or subtraction) element could be used in conjunction with our RNA detection scheme we created a DNA circuit consisting of three modules: a translator gate that connects the output strand from the assisted hybridization reaction to the threshold element, an annihilator gate and a single-stranded reference oligonucleotide that together act as the threshold element, and a catalytic reporter that amplifies any signal exceeding the threshold value to a constant level, allowing for a yes/no answer (Supplementary Fig. 5).

We tested this molecular thresholding system on three different transcripts (hTERT, EGFR, GAPDH) commonly used as biomarkers or reference genes for diagnostic purposes. To accommodate different RNAs, only the hybridization probe and helper strands needed to be switched, while all other strand displacement components are retained, demonstrating the modularity of the design. Each mRNA was individually transcribed in vitro from a complementary DNA (cDNA) template and quantified. For each transcript, we evaluated four experimental conditions using thermal annealing with varying ratios of transcript to reference oligonucleotide. Steady-state fluorescence values were acquired 2 h after addition of a catalytic amplifier and fluorescent reporter. With all three transcripts, we only observed an increase in fluorescence when the amount of transcript exceeded the amount of threshold.

A two-gene diagnostic classifier. For an experimental test of a full two-input classifier circuit, we selected hTERT, a cancer biomarker, as the target (associated with a positive weight) and GAPDH, a common internal reference gene in RT–qPCR experiments as the reference RNA (associated with a negative weight) (Fig. 3b). Relative quantitation of HTERT to GAPDH in human plasma has been suggested as an early diagnostic and prognostic biomarker in human cancer. The thresholding (subtraction) and amplification reaction are performed exactly as above, but, instead of an external reference strand to set the threshold value, there now is an internal reference RNA associated with a negative weight that effectively sets a threshold (Supplementary Fig. 6).

We evaluated four classifiers with an hTERT weight of +1 and GAPDH weights of −1, −2, −3 and −4 (Fig. 3c). A sample containing both RNA transcripts was first combined with corresponding hybridization probes and helper strands. hTERT transcript was present at 15 nM while GAPDH transcript was titrated from 0 nM to 14 nM with all DNA circuits components added at higher, non-limiting concentrations. We also characterized a classifier response with an hTERT weight of +1 and GAPDH weight of −2 with a range of concentrations of each transcript (0 nM to 20 nM) (Fig. 3d,e). Overall, we evaluated 64 different experimental conditions where we recorded fluorescence levels for 2 h after addition of strand displacement components. We only observed a significant increase in fluorescence in conditions when the amount of hTERT transcript was above the threshold set by the product of the GAPDH transcript concentration and weight, in agreement with the classifier design.

Training a multi-gene SVM. We next sought to scale up our molecular classifier framework. Discriminating between viral and bacterial infections using molecular gene expression classification is a promising application because it requires a rapid, cost-effective and self-contained process to be implemented in a clinical setting. In 2016, a peripheral whole-blood gene expression classifier with 130 genes was developed to differentiate between bacterial infections, viral infections, non-infectious illness and healthy controls with 87% accuracy10.

To build a molecular classifier, we first simplified the classification problem by distinguishing only between viral and bacterial infections. We used the publicly available gene expression data corresponding to 115 viral infections and 70 bacterial infections for classifier training10. For each patient, gene expression values for 14,500 human genes were measured. We implemented an SVM to determine the minimal set of genes and corresponding weights for this classification problem. This process involved iterating through multiple sets of features (genes) and associated weights until converging to a solution that resulted in the best classification outcome.

We trained an SVM algorithm with the following constraints: First we required a low number of genes (<10) to allow for the classifier to be implemented at the molecular level. Second, we constrained weights to integer values between −5 to +5. This choice was made to limit the number of probes for a single gene as well as the overall size of the classifier. Third, we made the misclassification penalty for bacterial samples three times higher than that for viral samples. This choice was made because the worst possible outcome is to incorrectly diagnose a bacterial infection as viral, delaying the use of antibiotics. Even though this classification model performed well in the validation set, it is important to note that a model with a higher number of features may be more robust when encountering gene expression variability absent in the training data set. We selected nine classifiers with at least 80% accuracy in the training set and validated them using a different gene expression data set. We selected the classification model with the highest performance in the validation set to build a molecular classifier (Fig. 4a). The selected classifier correctly labelled 94% and 80% of bacterial and viral samples in the training set and 89% of bacterial and 90% of viral samples in the validation set (Fig. 4b,c).

A molecular implementation of the bacterial vs viral classifier. Next, we designed a molecular implementation of the bacterial vs viral classifier. First, we selected regions in each transcript that consisted of individual exons that were at least 200 bp long such that they could fit multiple hybridization probes. Due to the large number of transcripts and associated probes, we implemented a probe design tool for systematically generating the necessary DNA components for molecular classification. Each transcript was assigned a number of hybridization probes and helper strands, based on the weights learned in silico. Positive and negative transcripts were assigned hybridization probes with different output domains such that the concentrations of the positive and negative output strands represent the weighted sums of the respective RNA inputs, as described above. The complete DNA classifier consists of 20 hybridization probes and 14 helper strands (two for each transcript). A strand displacement cascade using two translator gates and two fluorescent reporters aggregate the signal generated by the hybridization module. Overall, the circuit consists of 62 different oligonucleotides.

Rather than performing the subtraction at the molecular level as we have done in the previous example, we chose to use two distinct fluorophores to read out the positive and negative output strands individually, which allowed us to more quantitatively characterize the performance of individual classifier components. A fluorescent reporter containing a 6-FAM (fluorescein) (FAM) and a quencher was associated with positive/bacterial transcripts, while a fluorescent reporter containing a 6-carboxyl-X-rhodamine (ROX) and a quencher was associate with negative/viral transcripts (Fig. 5a). Upon reporter calibration, the fluorescence signal from the ROX reporter can be subtracted from the FAM reporter signal to obtain a normalized signal used for classification ([FAM] − [ROX] nM). Samples resulting in a normalized signal of [FAM] − [ROX] > 0 belong to the bacterial infection category, and samples for which this signal is less than zero belong to the viral infection category.

After assembling the molecular classifier, we first used synthetic DNA oligonucleotide targets to individually test all 20 hybridization probes. Upon thermal annealing and subsequent strand displacement, we confirmed that each oligonucleotide target triggered the intended fluorescent channel with the expected signal intensity (corresponding to a unit weight) while the signal remained near background in the other channel (Fig. 5b). Subsequently, we tested the molecular classifier using in vitro transcribed RNA species. After addition of each RNA transcript to the molecular classifier, we again measured the fluorescence response across both channels. For each transcript, we only observed significant increase in fluorescence in the expected channel. After calibration and subtraction of both channel fluorescence signals, we obtained a normalized signal for each transcript addition ([FAM] – [ROX] nM). We found this normalized signal to be proportional to the weight assigned to each gene, suggesting that the molecular weight implementation was performed correctly (Fig. 5c).

Finally, we tested our molecular classifier with samples containing RNA molecules matching the expression profiles from the training set microarray data. We selected 12 samples corresponding to six patients with viral and six patients with bacterial infections (Fig. 5d). We replicated the original gene expression profile by adding each cDNA amplicon based on its expected concentration as calculated from the microarray data. Each amplicon contained a T7 promoter for RNA transcription. Samples were then diluted to approximately 10 picomolar followed by in vitro transcription, which resulted in 1,000× amplification (Fig. 5e). As expected, upon addition of each sample to the molecular classifier, we observed significant triggering in both fluorescence channels. All samples were classified correctly based on the normalized signal intensity. Furthermore, we found a strong correlation between the normalized signal intensity and the corresponding computational output for each sample as estimated using the corresponding SVM model (Fig. 5f).

Discussion

We have introduced a systematic framework for translating an in silico gene expression classifier into DNA circuitry. We confirmed the robustness of this framework by building two distinct classifiers with varying numbers of weights and inputs. Using our approach, any in silico classifier can in principle be converted into a molecular classifier, synthesized for rapid prototyping and experimentally validated.

We developed three novel building blocks to enable molecular computation with RNA transcripts as inputs. First, breaking up transcript detection into two separate steps (assisted hybridization and strand displacement) enabled us to robustly perform molecular computing with any RNA transcript as an input. Second, by varying the number of probes that hybridize to an RNA transcript we were able to differentially weigh the importance of transcripts. Third, by designing probes with shared output sequences we were able to compute the weighted sum of multiple transcripts. So far, we have used these building blocks to create classifiers with up to seven distinct RNA inputs and up to five (positive or negative) probes per transcript. However, the size of the classifiers could in principle be scaled to tens or hundreds of targets with the number of weights only limited by the size of the transcripts. In principle, potential crosstalk between probes and incorrect targets becomes more likely when the number of probes is higher. Nevertheless, a thermodynamic simulation of these interactions can inform the selection of probes across the length of a target RNA transcript that exhibit little or no crosstalk.

Compared with existing methods for gene expression analysis, our approach is well suited to the inexpensive and rapid examination of clinical samples (Supplementary Table 5). Because of its experimental simplicity, our workflow is fast: the combined reaction time for the assisted hybridization module and strand displacement reaction was under 20 min with no additional time required for computational analysis and data interpretation. More fundamentally, the amount of work required to perform gene expression classification using our framework is independent of the number of genes in the assay. The complexity of RT–qPCR experiments, the current gold standard for gene expression profiling in the clinic, in contrast scales linearly with the number of genes being analysed. The DNA-based classification workflow thus dramatically reduces the need for liquid handling, making it a good fit for point-of-care applications. RNA sequencing and barcoded RNA hybridization (Nanostring) also allow for multiplexed gene expression analysis in a single reaction, but require expensive instrumentation or consumables. In contrast, we can perform expression analysis by harnessing DNA computation while relying on inexpensive instrumentation (a thermocycler and a fluorescence reader). Finally, all alternative approaches provide information about the expression of individual genes in a panel, while our approach aggregates this information at the molecular level and provides a single, easy-to-interpret diagnosis, enabling fast turnaround.

It should be noted, however, that the rate of the strand displacement reaction is highly dependent on the concentration of RNA inputs, and including a pre-amplification step in the workflow would increase the processing time. Here, we have demonstrated amplification of a mixture of cDNA amplicons in the low picomolar range using in vitro transcription before molecular classification. However, RNA transcripts are typically present at attomolar or femtomolar concentrations in tissue and blood RNA samples. Other amplification strategies, such as rolling-circle amplification or loop-mediated isothermal amplification, will need to be explored for further amplification and may be more suited for point-of-care applications. Moreover, the output of the classification can be measured using a different readout system such as a paper-based substrate or a colorimetric reaction to further increase the sensitivity or simplify readout of the results.

Still, by demonstrating a robust and modular approach for instrument-free analysis of complex gene expression signatures, our work fills an important gap in the existing toolbox for engineering affordable point-of-care diagnostics. The number of clinical studies examining how variations in peripheral gene expression are associated with disease diagnostics, monitoring and prognosis is ever increasing, and the use of molecular computation for gene expression analysis suggests a path towards translating this academic knowledge into future diagnostics.

Methods

DNA oligonucleotides. All DNA oligonucleotides were purchased from Integrated DNA Technology (IDT). Individual DNA oligonucleotides were suspended to 100 μM and stored in water. Fluorophore and quencher-labelled oligonucleotides were ordered HPLC-purified, except for <q> FAM-labelled oligonucleotides. Unlabelled oligonucleotides were unpurified.

Hybridization probe preparation. Hybridization probes consisted of annealed complex of two DNA oligonucleotides: a 21 nt bottom strand and a 56 nt top strand. The strands were mixed stoichiometrically with 30% excess of the bottom strand and then thermally annealed (heated to 98 °C for 10 s and cooled uniformly from 98 °C to 25 °C over the course of 73 min).

Hybridization probes for the viral/bacterial classifier. A total of 40 oligonucleotides (top and bottom strands) corresponding to 20 hybridization probes were ordered using IDT 25 nmol DNA Plate Oligo synthesis normalized to 100 μM on IDT LabReady buffer. For purification, 20 top strands and 20 bottom strands were pooled together, respectively, and purified as a mixture using 12% urea 19:1 acrylamide: bisacrylamide gel (SequaGel UreaGel System, National Diagnostics). Subsequently, gel bands were visualized using ultraviolet light with a fluorescent backplate, and then cut out and eluted into 1 ml 1 × TAE, 12.5 mM Mg2+ for 12 h. Concentrations were calculated by measuring absorbance at 260 nm (Eppendorf Biophotometer plus) and using an IDT-specified extinction coefficient.

Strand displacement probe preparation. Strand displacement probes (translators, reporters, catalytic amplifiers and annihilator gates) consisted of annealed complexes of two or more DNA oligonucleotides. The strands were mixed stoichiometrically with 10% excess of the target binding strand for the translator, catalytic amplifier gate and annihilator gate. Subsequently, DNA complexes were thermally annealed (heated to 98 °C for 10 s and cooled uniformly from 98 °C to 25 °C over the course of 73 min). After annealing, individual probes were purified using a 12% non-denaturing PAGE gel as described above.

Cellular mRNA preparation. Cellular mRNA was extracted from the HEK293 (ATCC 30-2003) human cell line using a magnetic isolation kit for mRNA (NEB Next Poly(A) mRNA Magnetic Isolation kit #E7490). Cellular mRNA was aliquoted and stored in nuclease-free water with RNAse inhibitor (NEB) at −80 °C until needed.

RNA target preparation. Amplicons corresponding to RNA target sequences were generated by PCR amplification of HEK293 cDNA or human genomic DNA (ThermoFisher catalogue no. 4312660). Amplification of each target was carried out with a corresponding forward primer containing a T7 RNA polymerase promoter sequence (5-TAATACGACTCACTATAGGG-3). After amplification, each product was visualized on a 1.5% agarose gel and the correct band was excised and processed with a gel extraction kit (QIAGEN catalogue no. 28704). RNA targets were generated using a T7 RiboMAX Express Large-Scale RNA Production System (Promega). Purification of RNA targets was carried out using a phenol/ chloroform extraction protocol. Final RNA concentrations were determined using absorbance at 260 nm and an estimated extinction coefficient for the corresponding single-stranded RNA. RNA was aliquoted and stored in nuclease-free water with RNAse inhibitor (NEB) at −80 °C until needed.

Time-course fluorescence measurements. For experiments using individual transcripts, kinetic fluorescence measurements were performed using a Horiba FluoroMax 3 spectrofluorometer and Hellma Semi-Micro 114F cuvettes. An external temperature bath maintained the reaction temperature at 25 °C. A four-sample changer was used so that time-based fluorescence experiments were performed in groups of four. For experiments related to comparison across multiple transcripts (for example, hTERT vs GAPDH classifier, viral vs bacterial classifier), kinetic fluorescence measurements were performed using a fluorescence plate reader for higher measurement throughput (Biotek Synergy HTX). Thermal annealing and strand displacement reactions were carried out in $1 \times$ TAE, 12.5 mM Mg^{2+}.

Fluorescence normalization. Arbitrary fluorescence units were converted to concentrations using a calibration curve of each reporter complex. To create a calibration curve, annealed reporter complex stock was suspended in $1 \times$ TAE/ Mg^{2+} and an initial baseline fluorescence signal was recorded. This was followed by stepwise addition of known concentrations of reporter triggering strands. After each trigger strand addition, the steady state was recorded.

Viral/bacterial SVM training and validation. To train the SVM algorithm, we obtained microarray data (NCBI GSE63990) for 273 ill patients and 44 healthy volunteers. We processed the data set by first selecting samples labelled only as bacterial or viral infections (70 and 115 samples, respectively) and transforming the microarray gene expression ratios by logarithm (base 2) to estimate biological expression levels. We trained an SVM algorithm (classifier with a linear kernel) on this data set to distinguish between viral and bacterial classes using the SVM. Linear SVC function from Python library sklearn. We used a squared hinge loss function with L1 norm while iterating through multiple penalty parameters to obtain SVM classifiers with a varying number of features. We found nine models that employed fewer than ten genes while maintaining a classification accuracy of 80% or higher in the training set. We evaluated these classifiers using a different microarray data set (NCBI GSE6269) where they performed similarly well (area under the curve (AUC) > 0.90). Finally, we selected the classifier with the highest AUC value for experimental implementation.

Computational tool for generating hybridization probes from the in silico classifier. First, we generated an input file containing each transcript sequence and their corresponding weights from the in silico classifier. A python script sliced the transcript sequence to generate helper strands (first and last 60 nt), hybridization targets (30 nt each) and hybridization probes. Hybridization probes were generated with either a positive or negative sequence domain based on the classifier weight. The output of this script contains each component sequence (helper, top strand hybridization probe, bottom strand hybridization probe and target sequence) and name.

Reporting Summary. Further information on experimental design is available in the Nature Research Reporting Summary linked to this article.

Code availability. Computer code used in the computational sections of this work is available in the GitHub repository (https://github.com/rmlb/classifier_probegen/) or from the corresponding author upon request.

Data availability. Characterization data and experimental protocols for this work are available within this manuscript and its associated Supplementary Information, or from the corresponding author upon request.